THE STORY OF

LONGHORNS

FOOTBALL

HORNS!
A HISTORY

MARK WANGRIN

A FIRESIDE BOOK
PUBLISHED BY SIMON & SCHUSTER

NEW YORK LONDON TORONTO SYDNEY

FIRESIDE
Rockefeller Center
1230 Avenue of the Americas
New York, NY 10020

For information about special discounts for bulk purchases,
please contact Simon & Schuster Special Sales at
1-800-456-6798 or business@simonandschuster.com.

Designed by Ruth Lee-Mui

Manufactured in the United States of America

1   3   5   7   9   10   8   6   4   2

Library of Congress Cataloging-in-Publication Data is available.

ISBN-13: 978-0-7432-9718-9
ISBN-10   0-7432-9718-0

To Mom and Dad, for always believing

CONTENTS

HORNS!

A HISTORY

THE STORY OF
LONGHORNS FOOTBALL

1

A DREAM TO LIVE

Everything anybody needed to know about the essence of football at the University of Texas was represented at the end of a bunch of six-inch burnt-orange plastic numbers on the wall of the auditorium at the University of Texas's Moncrief-Neuhaus Athletics Complex. Under the heading "National Championships" and following the years "1963, 1969, 1970" was a lonely comma. It reflected everything that was expected to be accomplished by the

Vince Young's fourth-down touchdown scramble ended 35 years of frustration.

prideful Longhorns football program. And everything that hadn't.

It may have been the most pregnant pause in college football.

When Coach Mack Brown had it affixed there, during a multimillion-dollar facility renovation in 1998, it represented more than hope. It stood for expectations, the expectations that Brown, a homespun Tennessean who embraced all that Texas stood for, would return the Longhorns to the national spotlight. It was Mack Brown's blessing to be at a school with the arrogance, tradition, and means necessary to hang that comma, but it sometimes seemed more like a curse.

It had been thirty-five years since the Longhorns last celebrated a national title; thirty-six since it had been undisputed. On December 6, 1969, when the Longhorns beat Arkansas in Fayetteville in the Big Shootout, the school was guaranteed at least a share of its second national title. Fans swarmed Austin's Guadalupe Street, known locally as the Drag, hugging strangers and flashing "Hook 'em Horns" signs. Car horns bleated and the crowds belted out choruses of "Texas! Fight!" Ten thousand fans greeted the team at the airport, a crush so intense the players couldn't even leave the plane for almost a half hour.

A month later, when the Longhorns beat Notre Dame in the Cotton Bowl to win the second half of that title, the Associated Press crown, there was more celebration. A year later the Longhorns ran their winning streak to 30 with a 42–7 romp over Arkansas in what was billed as "The Big Shootout II" at Memorial Stadium, a moment that guaranteed the UPI national title. Losing the Cotton Bowl in a rematch with a Notre Dame team more prepared to defense the wish-

bone forced a split title, but Orange-bloods everywhere reveled in the Longhorns' delicious run.

Even before the celebration died down, though, the architect of the two national titles sounded a cautionary note. "Next year we'll be back with the regular folk," Coach Darrell K Royal said on his weekly television show, but few believed him.

They were Texas, the flagship university in a state whose people, by nature, don't take the backseat. They take the keys. If a Texan hasn't mentioned that the state is the only one in the union that once flew its own flag as a sovereign nation, it's just because he's being polite. Or he's sleeping.

They knew they would be celebrating again, and soon.

Thirty-five years later, they were still waiting. Royal, worn down by the changing emphasis on recruiting, had retired. Three coaches had come and gone. Five American presidents had come and gone. Governments were toppled. Tectonic plates moved. Continents were formed. Galaxies were created. Or so it seemed.

The Longhorns had entered the final game of the season twice with a shot at the national title, in 1977 and 1983, only to watch both fade, one with a rout by Notre Dame; one with a muffed punt that should have never happened.

Meanwhile, some of the game's traditional powers had rebounded from lower lows to win national titles. Oklahoma, two years removed from a streak of five nonwinning seasons, routed the Longhorns 66–14 in their annual showdown in Dallas in 2000 on its way to a 13–2 upset victory over Florida State in the Orange Bowl and the Sooners' seventh national title. A year later it was Ohio State hoisting the Bowl Championship Series (BCS) trophy, and then LSU and Southern Cal. Getting left in the dust only made the Longhorns' longing more acute.

Some of the Longhorn players never noticed the comma. Some couldn't avoid it. "Some of the coaches would tell us, there's a comma on the wall and nothing after it," guard Justin Blalock said. "They wanted us to put something up there. They were joking. But they were serious."

Texas got serious on the long road back to the top when it hired Mack Brown in December 1997. As is the way with coaching hires, it was a polar swing that followed a polar swing that followed a polar swing, all trying to replace the guy that didn't work with his exact opposite.

It began when Royal retired in 1976. Uncomfortable with a coach who was a folksy, laid-back friend of long-haired musicians, former governor Allan Shivers, then chairman of the Board of Regents, and university president Lorene Rogers denied Royal a legend's right—to name his own successor—and opted for

*President Bush welcomed
the national champions
to the White House.*

another self-made man. But this one was high-energy and highly organized and even more buttoned down, former Longhorn assistant Fred Akers.

Akers flirted with two national titles, only to have self-inflicted wounds cost them both shots in Cotton Bowls they were favored to win. When recruiting headed south, with many alumni leading the way by telling recruits to stay away, Akers was doomed.

In came the obvious choice, the man who played for Darrell, coached with Darrell, wore boots and drawled homespun quips like Darrell. But David McWilliams wasn't Darrell, and all the goodwill in the Longhorn universe couldn't save him after he followed up a breakthrough Southwest Conference championship season in 1990 with a 4–7 record in 1991.

And so the pendulum swung. John Mackovic didn't know a taco from a two-step and didn't much care to learn the difference. He wore ties and pressed shirts and did local advertisements for a high-dollar men's clothier. He collected wines, once telling a reporter the perfect team was like a vintage Chateau Petrus.

Mackovic's teams often played like a Chateau Petrus. Just as often they were Boone's Farm. His Longhorns shared the Southwest Conference title in 1994, won it outright with a gutsy victory at Texas A&M the following year, and then shocked the college football oddsmakers by stunning three-touchdown favorite

Nebraska in the first Big 12 championship game. They also lost by 63 points to UCLA and fell to Rice for the first time in 29 games.

Unlike the beloved McWilliams, Mackovic's icy ways and aversion to Longhorn tradition earned him zero goodwill, and when his team lost seven games the year after the Big 12 championship, he was reassigned.

Then the pendulum swung back and it pointed straight toward the 48-year-old Brown, a lifelong college football fan who said he teared up when he heard the classic school fight songs. Brown smartly and genuinely embraced Longhorn tradition, welcomed back the lettermen and high school coaches to practice, and developed the concept of Longhorns as family so deftly that he rarely uttered a sentence that didn't mention either his wife Sally or Coach Royal or how he hugged some player's neck.

And then he went ahead and hung that comma.

Actually, the sign makers first hung a period there. They did the same thing on the other wall, after the list of conference champions. Brown made them change it as quickly as they could.

"I thought a period was way too final," Brown said.

He then explained the message behind it.

"What I felt was the players needed to understand it's not a matter of if, it's a matter of when," he said. "And our staff needed to understand that, too. In life if you can't dream you have no chance. So that comma, in some ways was subtle pressure. In other ways a motivator that it could happen and in the third way a dream that it would happen."

The expectations it represented meant that when the Longhorns failed to meet them, somebody had to get the blame. Brown's wife Sally told him in no uncertain terms who that was.

"It's funny," Brown said. "In times that people were griping because we

Tickets to the Rose Bowl were selling for upwards of $4,000 apiece.

JANUARY 4, 2006

Rose Bowl Game

BOWL CHAMPIONSHIP SERIES

citi

NATIONAL CHAMPIONSHIP
4:30 PM [PREGAME ACTIVITIES] ■ TOTAL PRICE $175.00

GATE	TUNNEL	ROW	SEAT
	1	4	06

GATE	TUNNEL	ROW	SEAT
	1	4	06

GATE CHECK VOID IF DETACHED ■ 92ND ROSE BOWL GAME - WEDNESDAY, JANUARY 4, 2006

were 11–2, I think even Sally told me, 'You're the reason, because you put that comma up there and you constantly talk about winning the national championship and they're frustrated you haven't done it.' So there's a fine line between what the goal is, what the dream is and actuality."

One of the Longhorns' prime mottos in 2005 was "Living the Dream." It was a dream the Longhorns long held, but ask Brown when he thinks it was germinated and he points back to the 2004 season and what looked to be one of the Longhorns' all-time low points.

It was November 6, and the Longhorns had worked their way up to No. 6 in the Associated Press poll four weeks after losing to Oklahoma for the fifth straight time. No. 19 Oklahoma State came to Texas Royal-Memorial Stadium that evening, which was clear and unusually warm.

The Cowboys wasted no time in making it hotter, breaking open an early 7–7 tie by scoring four quick touchdowns, including two on drives of three plays or less to go up 35–7 with just over a minute left in the first half. The Longhorns scored on a 5-yard pass from Vince Young to Bo Scaife with only 3 seconds left in the first half but they still trailed 35–14 heading into the locker room.

That's when Brown first remembered seeing the pieces come together.

"It would have been an easy time for

our fans to boo us out of the stadium, which I'm sure Texas fans have done before, from what I could tell," Brown said. "Our players could have quit and our coaches could have panicked and I was amazed as we were leaving the field after we scored to make it 35–14 our fans were cheering for us. I usually don't hear [cheering during games] and I heard that and thought, Wow, that's unique. And when we went into the locker room the coaches were so calm and confident and the players went out and dominated."

Brown, borrowing a page from Royal's book of motivational ploys, took advantage of the name-your-score atmosphere and did just that. He went to the chalkboard and wrote: 42–35.

"They don't know who we are," Brown told his team. "We're going to go out and score on our first drive and we're going to win 42–35."

After a second half that featured six unanswered touchdowns, four by halfback Cedric Benson, and that culminated in a 56–35 victory, the greatest comeback in school history, Brown had something else to say to his team.

"I apologized," Brown said, "for underestimating them."

Brown saw an attitude that hadn't always been around.

"Our guys played to a different level in the second half," Brown said. "We could have called anything on offense in the second half, and it would have worked. We could have called anything on defense, and it would've worked, too. The offense started the momentum change, and the defense fed off of it.

"Shoot, this wasn't adversity. This was

Texas fans don't wear their hearts only on their sleeves.

a train wreck. We were splattered and scattered at halftime."

Revived, the Longhorns still lived dangerously. The following week they went up to Lawrence to play a 3–6 Kansas team that boasted a stout rushing defense but had injury-induced inconsistency at quarterback. Texas led 13–9 heading into the third quarter, but the 22-point underdog Jayhawks struck quickly on scoring drives of 5 and 4 plays and led 23–13 with less than eight minutes left in the game.

It was time for more Vince Young heroics. Young led the Longhorns on an 87-yard drive that he capped with an 18-yard touchdown run with 4:32 left.

It appeared Young wouldn't get a chance to complete the comeback when Kansas backup quarterback Brian Luke found Charles Gordon for a 16-yard gain on third-and-seven at the Jayhawks' 26 with 2:32 left, which would have allowed Kansas to all but run out the clock. But Gordon was flagged for pushing off on UT cornerback Tarell Brown, and Jayhawks Coach Mark Mangino was livid on the sidelines.

Kansas then ran a dive on third-and-20 from the 13, lost a yard, and Kyle Tucker's punt wobbled out of bounds at the Jayhawks' 47.

The Longhorn drive appeared stalled at their own 45, when they faced fourth-and-18. Young sent all his receivers deep and, unable to find anyone open, he darted to his left and outran linebacker Nick Reid for 22 yards and first down.

Reid and Young had a running verbal battle during the game and Reid made his case with a game-high 14 tackles, but his diving try to trip up Young fell inches short on a move Young called "The Texas Two-Step."

"I refuse to let that guy make that tackle, especially when it's one-on-one," Young said. "In my head, I was already going through making that guy miss when I saw we were one-on-one. That guy was talking trash the whole game. I got the last word on him."

Four plays later Young took advantage of a full blitz and man-to-man coverage to loft a 21-yard touchdown pass to Tony Jeffrey in the left corner of the end zone with 11 seconds left for a 27–23 victory.

Mangino groused that the call was the result of league officials wanting to get a second team in the BCS—and the $4 million that went with it. "You know what this is all about, don't you?" Mangino said. "It's called BCS. That's what made a difference today. That's what made the difference on that call in front of their bench—dollar signs."

Mangino later retracted his comments, but the Longhorns wouldn't soon forget.

Texas closed the regular season with a 26–13 victory over Texas A&M, after which Mack Brown made a not-so-subtle plea that poll voters switch allegiances and move the Longhorns ahead of Cal, which was in position to gain the last at-large BCS berth.

"If you've got a vote, vote for us," Brown appealed to AP voters at his postgame media conference. "I'm asking you to do that and I'm asking everyone across the nation. This team deserves to be in the BCS. They deserve to go more than some teams that are being talked about."

The voters listened. Texas crept to within .0013 computer points of Cal in the BCS poll released two days later and then, after Cal beat Southern Mississippi 26–16 in unspectacular fashion the following week, the Longhorns leapfrogged the Golden Bears. Six coaches in the ESPN/USA Today Coaches Poll dropped the Bears, who weren't below six on any of the previous ballots, to seventh or eighth.

Columnist and AP voter Neal McCready of the *Mobile Register* bumped Texas from No. 9 to No. 5, conceding he'd been deluged by calls, e-mails, and letters from Longhorn fans wanting him to change. In a subsequent column that explained his change of heart McCready wrote, "I fixed it today, moving the Longhorns to No. 5. Please leave me alone now, you're scaring my wife."

While the controversy flared, the Longhorns prepared for unfamiliar ground. Texas finally had its first BCS berth in school history—the Bowl Alliance was the format used when the Longhorns won the Big 12 title in 1996

and went to the Fiesta Bowl—and was scheduled to meet Michigan, a team it had never faced.

The Longhorns had never seen the Wolverines, but the Wolverines had never seen what Young could do if given running lanes. They dared Young to beat them and he obliged, running for 192 yards and a Rose Bowl–record four touchdowns. Young also completed 16 of 28 passes for 180 yards and a touchdown.

Young's fourth touchdown, from 23 yards, put Texas up 35–34 but Steve Breaston returned the ensuing kickoff 53 yards, one of four he had longer than 40 yards, to set up a 42-yard Garrett Rivas field goal that put Michigan up 37–35 with 3:04 left.

With Young running on keepers and scrambles, the Longhorns moved to the Michigan 19, where they milked the clock down to 2 seconds before Dusty Mangum kicked the game-winning 37-yard field goal at the gun.

Overcome with excitement after the 38–37 victory, Brown said, "There'll never be a better game in the Rose Bowl. There may be some as good, but there won't be any better."

After receiving his Outstanding Offensive Play Award on the hastily erected stage, Young was asked during the postgame interview on ABC if he wanted to come back the next year. The Rose Bowl was set to host the BCS title game on January 4, 2006.

"We'll be back!" Young screamed,

Longhorn über-fan Matthew McConaughey cheers a Mike Jones touchdown against Nebraska in 1999.

shooting his hand into the air in an emphatic "Hook 'em."

"When Vince said we'd be back he wasn't lying," safety Michael Griffin said. "That's when it all started. At first we thought it was funny how he said it, because it sounded so country. But he said he was serious. When we got back to school, we watched the highlights and we saw it again."

And they, too, began believing. Young, meanwhile, finally had a team to call his own and he wasted no time in staking out his territory.

Before classes ended in the spring, Young set the tone for the summer and the season to come. The subject was the Longhorns' informal evening seven-on-seven workouts at Frank Denius Fields.

"We're going to be out there on Tuesday and Thursday at seven o'clock," Young told his teammates. "If you're not there, don't worry about showing up during two-a-days. We don't need you."

Said Griffin, "Everybody showed up. We could see he was a true leader. Everybody trusted him."

Texas opened the 2005 season at home against Louisiana-Lafayette, ranked No. 2 in both preseason polls behind defending champion Southern Cal. While the Longhorns were hoping to find answers to who would replace 2005 first-round NFL picks Benson and linebacker Derrick Johnson, the Ragin' Cajuns were trying to regroup after fleeing Hurricane Katrina.

Texas rolled 60–3, getting a promising effort from Benson heir apparent Jamaal Charles, a speedy freshman from Port Arthur, while operating from a limited play list. A visit to Ohio State was next, and Brown didn't want to show anything he didn't have to show.

"It was the perfect opening game," he said.

Texas had never played Ohio State, either, though had there been a BCS in place in 1970 the Longhorns and Buckeyes would have met for the national title. Instead, Texas went to the Cotton Bowl, where it lost to Notre Dame, and Ohio State fell to Southern Cal in the Rose Bowl.

Ohio Stadium, known widely as the Horseshoe, is one of college football's

Vince Young's heroics against Michigan in the 2005 Rose Bowl cemented his role as team leader.

most venerable and scenic venues. It is also one of the loudest, and the 105,565 who packed it on September 10 for the prime-time ABC game had a long morning and afternoon of tailgating to prepare to see the No. 4 Buckeyes extend their home winning streak over nonconference foes past 36.

"That place was ridiculous, the worst I'd ever been to," Blalock said. "I couldn't hear myself think. The best we could do was point or gesture. There was no verbal communication, even in the huddle. Sometimes you'd get the play from the guy next to you."

Texas was plagued by turnovers early, but the Longhorn defense managed to take some of the fire out of the crowd by holding the Buckeyes to five field goals, four on possessions that started inside the Longhorns 40-yard line.

When Josh Huston kicked a 26-yard field goal with 5:12 left in the third quarter it gave the Buckeyes a 22–16 lead. With a chance to put the game away with four minutes left, he was barely wide right.

"Thanks for coming," one Buckeyes fan yelled to a Fiesta Bowl official on the sideline, "but we're going to the Rose Bowl."

Now it was Young's turn. Though Ohio State linebacker Bobby Carpenter had said the week before that it was the Buckeyes' goal to have Young leave Columbus no longer a Heisman candidate, Young was now to vault himself higher into the race. Texas, 67 yards away from the go-ahead touchdown, went to its potent no-huddle attack. Converting a third-and-6 with a 9-yard pass to Charles and a third-and-1 with a quarterback sneak, Young moved the team to the Ohio State 24-yard line.

Young took the shotgun snap, faked a handoff to Charles, and looked to his left, first at tight end David Thomas and then wide receiver Limas Sweed heading toward the corner of the end zone against a zone that left him with only one defender nearby. Young threw and free safety Nate Salley was late getting over, allowing Sweed to make a backwards, falling catch for the touchdown. A late team safety sealed the win.

"We just never stopped believing," said Sweed, who had his first career touchdown catch. "We knew we were going to get it done."

"We had been through this before," Young said of the late-game heroics. "I'm pretty much used to it now."

Now came a bit of unfinished business. Texas hadn't beaten Oklahoma in five seasons, in the process enduring 49- and 52-point routs and a shutout that ended the nation's longest scoring streak. The 2005 Sooners had lost a talented senior class and were relying on a freshman, Rhett Bomar, at quarterback. They came into the game at 2–2, having lost to TCU and UCLA, and few figured they'd give the Longhorns a battle.

They didn't. The Longhorns scored

facing page: Limas Sweed's acrobatic touchdown against Ohio State kept the title dream alive.

their most points ever against Oklahoma and matched their largest margin of victory in the fiery 100-year history of the rivalry.

Young, who had struggled against Oklahoma his first two seasons, passed for 241 yards and three touchdowns. Texas rolled up 444 yards total offense, led by Charles's 116 yards rushing. Defensively, the Longhorns held the Sooners, who got only limited snaps from injured 2004 Heisman Trophy runner-up Adrian Peterson, to only 171 yards total offense.

When the final gun sounded, the Longhorns took turns trying on the Golden Hat trophy that went to the winning team and Vince Young took a victory lap, dancing his way around the front row of the Texas end of the Cotton Bowl, slapping fives with and getting hugged by jubilant fans.

Brown, who drew heavy doses of criticism during the drought, didn't publicly allow himself to revel in the victory.

"I don't think this team has near played its best game," Brown said. "That's the exciting part."

After the Oklahoma game, Longhorn fans began talking Rose Bowl in earnest and making their plans to spend January 4 in Pasadena, booking flights and searching the Internet for ticket deals.

"We'd be in class and run into kids who'd tell us, 'I'm going to California, got my reservations, I'm going,'" tackle Justin Blalock recalled. "I'm like, 'You

know we've only played five games.' I'd be thinking to myself, it would really suck if you end up seeing two other teams play."

What faced the Longhorns was an end of the regular season stretch run that looked far from dangerous. The Longhorns easily handled Colorado before ripping the only ranked team left on their schedule, No. 10 Texas Tech, 52–17 at home. Then came a visit to Oklahoma State, where the Cowboys again jumped out, this time to a 28–9 halftime lead, only to have the Young-led Longhorns roar back to score 38 unanswered points and win 47–28.

Last up was Texas A&M. When Brown was a halfback at Florida State, his backfield coach was Bill Parcells. The two kept in touch as they climbed their respective coaching ladders and during the open week before the Longhorns would face Texas A&M, the Dallas Cowboys head coach sent his former player an e-mail. The message was a familiar one for Brown, reminding him of a saying he and fellow Seminoles assistant Dan Henning like to use to keep their players from getting too cocky.

They referred to too much positive press and fan adulation as "poison cheese."

The e-mail read, in part, "Everybody's bragging on them. Don't let them eat the cheese."

"And I remembered the story," Brown said. "There's a lot of poison cheese out there and it's dangling in front of you and everybody's bragging on you, with a good smell, and trying to get you to bite the poisoned cheese. Don't intoxicate yourself with poison."

When the Longhorns went to College Station the day after Thanksgiving they not only took the cheese, they seemed to ask for seconds. A&M was missing its star quarterback, Reggie McNeal, and was forced to play a talented but unproven freshman in Stephen McGee. A&M's defense was also not up to the Aggies' usual standards and the team was far from imposing, with an overtime victory over Baylor, a team the Longhorns had blanked 62–0 only twenty days earlier.

A&M ran the ball effectively early and got sterling play from McGee, and led the Longhorns 22–21 in the third quarter.

"I told them at halftime, I don't think you ate the cheese but some of you have been nibbling it," Brown said. "And they understood."

Texas drove 80 yards for a Ramonce Taylor touchdown run and then a punt blocked by Michael Griffin was returned for a touchdown by Cedric Griffin as the Longhorns survived 40–29.

Young's Heisman hopes, however, did not. Certain that he needed another superlative performance to keep pace with Southern Cal's Reggie Bush atop the Heisman polls, Young failed to thrive on a big stage for the first time since the 2004 Oklahoma game. He appeared to press too hard against the 109th-rated defense in the country and had his worst game, with a season low 181 yards total offense.

Texas had not only survived a potential ambush, but the victory over the Ag-

Sweed's one-handed catch helped the Longhorns pour it on Colorado.

COLORADO 3

gies provided Brown with the perfect motivation for the Big 12 championship game the following week at Reliant Stadium in Houston.

Over the years Texas alum Matthew McConaughey had become a frequent visitor to Longhorn practices, and knowing his youthful, Hollywood swagger appealed to the players, Brown had him speak to the team at practice that Thursday before they left for Houston.

"He told them, 'Get your goal on Saturday and your dream on January 4,'" Brown recalled. "And that really fit. So I didn't have to say anything after that. That's pretty much what we said before the game."

Facing Texas was a chance to recast history. In 2001, the Longhorns entered the Big 12 championship game in their home state, in Dallas, against a Colorado team they had beaten easily at home in midseason. Chris Simms turned the ball over four times and was replaced by Major Applewhite, but the Longhorns' furious rally fell short. It cost them a spot in the Bowl Championship Series championship game against Miami.

This time it wasn't even close. The Longhorns scored touchdowns on 9 of their first 10 possessions—not including a blocked punt they recovered in the end zone as part of a 21-point eruption during the first 5:01 of the third quarter. Texas won 70–3 in the most lopsided championship game in the history of any conference.

Tackle Justin Blalock is the first to say he's not the sentimental sort. But he couldn't help but appreciate what had unfolded. "We did a lot of absorbing that day," Blalock said. "Being Texas, we had the lion's share of the fans there. It was great seeing all the fans, knowing we had the first chance to go to the national championship game in a number of years."

One section of Texas fans celebrated so heartily, reaching out to the players as they ran past, that the front rail gave way, spilling them onto the Reliant Stadium field.

"Ain't no party but a Longhorn party," Vince Young said, sticking a rose behind his ear as the Longhorns paraded Coach Mack Brown's first conference title trophy in 22 seasons as a head coach.

"I voted Texas No. 1 all season, and they did nothing to change my vote," said Colorado Coach Gary Barnett. In the ultimate of ironies, five days after the embarrassing loss Barnett, whose program had been investigated on everything from unproven rape charges to misuse of summer camp funds, was forced out at Colorado. When the Longhorns had gone looking for a coach to replace Mackovic they first turned their attention to Barnett, who had worked miracles at Northwestern in leading the Wildcats to back-to-back Big Ten titles in 1995 and '96, before realizing Brown was the better fit.

Texas's victory over Colorado was the most lopsided of any conference title game to date.

"The first thing I thought is I didn't want to embarrass Colorado and Gary," Brown said. "I never saw a team play that well. We did everything right and it snowballed on them. The second thing is I didn't want everybody bragging on our team so much from the Colorado game to the national championship game that we forgot who we were and had to go back and work. So I was really pleased when we were walking off the field and they announced Reggie Bush had 175 yards in the first half and USC's up 55–14 because I thought that would at least counterbalance what had happened in our game."

USC would go on to crush crosstown rival UCLA 66–19, with Reggie Bush running for 260 yards and becoming the clear Heisman Trophy favorite. It also gave college football the game it had been waiting for since the Associated

The title shot that Texas fans had waited for since 1984 finally arrives in Pasadena.

Longhorn fans saw only one way to satisfy their sweet tooth—taking on No. 1 Southern California in the Rose Bowl.

Press and ESPN/USA Today Coaches polls first ranked USC No. 1 and Texas No. 2 in the preseason.

For Brown, it was an ending that had long eluded him. In 2001 Texas lost to Oklahoma at midseason, 14–3, but got a spot in the Big 12 championship game when the Sooners were bumped off at home by Oklahoma State the day after the Longhorns had finished their regular season by topping Texas A&M. They wasted that opportunity, losing 39–37 to Colorado, a team they had beaten by 34 in the regular season.

In 2002, after another midseason loss to the Sooners, they scrapped their way back to the No. 4 ranking, but their defense couldn't contain Texas Tech's passing game and they lost a shootout 42–38 to fall out of the BCS picture. In 2003 a two-loss Longhorn team was at No. 6 and poised to get an at-large BCS berth but Kansas State upset Oklahoma in the Big 12 championship game, sending the Wildcats to the Fiesta Bowl and the Longhorns to the Holiday Bowl, where they lost to Washington State.

Then came the breakthrough year of 2004, but the victory over Michigan only allowed the Longhorns to move up to No. 5.

"When you get to the end and don't finish it like you want to, it's frustrating," Brown said. "But as a coach, you know how close you are."

Now, with roses blooming again, and a spot in the BCS championship game at last, everybody knew the answer: one game.

2

HOORAY, VARSITY

The game was hyped like no other before it. It featured defending champion versus the challenger, and the media treated it as such. "Never before in the history of the university has there been such enthusiasm manifested in any one game as is now shown," read the front-page story in Austin's main daily. There were lineups and position breakdowns and insights into coaching strategies and predictions and, for those out of touch, a breakdown of the rules of the game.

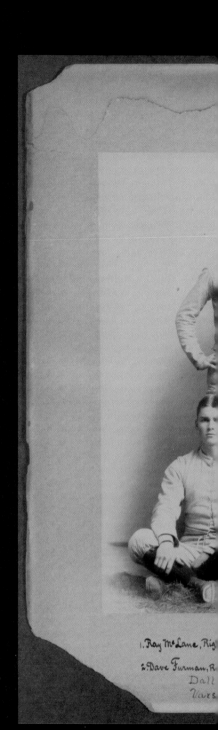

1. Ray McLane, Rig
2. Dave Furman, R
Dall
Vars

Foot-Ball Team - University of Texas, 1893-94.

ight End.   4. Victor Moore, Right Guard.   6. . . Meyer, Centre.   9. R. E. L. Roy, Left Tackle.
    3. James Morrison, Right Tackle.   7. Paul McLane, Cap't. Left End.   10. J. W. Philip, Left Guard.
Right Half   5. W. P. McLean, Quarter   8. Walter Crawford, Manager.   11. Rich'd. U. Lee, Left Half.
las, Nov. 30. 93.   1c. Ha. Day, Full Back.   Austin. Dec. 16. 93.
sity. 18. Dallas 16.   Varsity. 10 San Antonio 0.

This was the atmosphere in Austin and Dallas heading into the Thanksgiving weekend in November 1893, as the University of Texas sent its first organized football team into action against the Dallas Foot Ball Club at a field that was not far from where Fair Park and the Cotton Bowl now stand.

Football was first played at Rutgers in 1869 and the fast-paced, physical sport began appealing to universities throughout the East. Rapidly it spread westward through curious news accounts and former players looking to spread the game. The sport was played at Texas as early as 1891, when two sides were chosen on campus, but their efforts received little attention.

The enrollment of brothers Paul and Ray McLane and James Morrison in the fall of 1893 gave the fledgling club a boost. All three had played football in the East, and they organized a team, with Paul McLane serving as coach and directing the daily 4:30 P.M. practices behind the newly constructed Chemical Lab.

Word spread and the Dallas club, which had a long streak of holding opponents scoreless and billed itself as state champion, issued an invitation for the university boys to come play them on Thanksgiving Day at Fairgrounds Park.

The Texas team prepared for the trip by playing an exhibition game on the Texas campus on November 11. The se-

lect team won 10–2, but the most noteworthy event came when the ball burst after being squeezed too hard by star player Al Jacks in a pileup and the game was delayed while a student rode back into town on a bicycle to purchase a replacement.

Financing was also a problem. A local haberdashery, Harrell & Wilcox, supplied $100 to cover food and lodging, and a ticket agent for the International & Great Northern Railway supplied the train tickets.

As the train rolled out of the Austin station shortly before midnight on Tuesday, the crowd gave the team a hearty send-off.

Halla-ba-loo, Hooray, Hooray
Halla-ba-loo, Hooray, Hooray
Hooray, Varsity
Varsity, Varsity, UTA.

Up in Dallas, the weather was in the 70s and a crowd of over 2,000, enormous for that era, packed the grandstands long before the 2:30 P.M. kickoff. It was expected to be quite a show. The management of the Union Pacific placed a special train at the disposal of fans from Fort Worth and a unique halftime performance was scheduled. "Another source of attraction between the two halves of the game will be the exhibition riding by the noted bicyclist, Mr. Tackerberry of Fort Worth, who will endeavor to lower the state records for the quarter, half and the mile," read the advance story in the *Dallas Morning News.*

Plenty was going on in the world and around Dallas that day. Confederate General H. B. Granbury's remains arrived by train in Fort Worth and were reburied in Granbury, 29 years following the anniversary of his burial after he was killed in battle in Franklin, Tennessee. In Russia, news broke that twenty Catholics were slaughtered by troops at a church and many more drowned while fleeing. In Washington, D.C., the U.S. House Ways and Means Committee was expected to confirm a proposed income tax on "the net increase of all corporations and a tax on successions and legacies," but a provision to levy an annual tax against all households earning at least $5,000 a year was struck down.

Despite the Texas team's inexperience and the Dallas club being the reigning state champion, a close game was anticipated. "The Texas University team is in the pink of condition, which will make the contest a trying one in every respect for which endurance will be put at its best test," wrote an account in the *Morning News.*

Led by Jacks and Morrison, the Longhorns powered down the field on the opening drive for a score and led 12–10 at halftime. During halftime the referee, Fred Shelley of the Austin Athletic Club, grew so weary of complaining by the Dallas players that he quit and a player from the Fort Worth club

who had been watching took his place.

The switch did not matter, as Texas quickly scored again and won 18–16.

"The University of Texas Football team wiped up the earth this evening with the Dallas eleven," began the story in the *Austin Daily Statesman.* "This is the first time that the latter club has ever been scored against, much less defeated."

And football, at the University of Texas, was born. The Varsity, as the team was called then, went on to win three more games that year, shutting out San Antonio twice and then beating Dallas 16–0 in a rematch played in Austin, leaving no doubt they were the new state champions.

Football took off in 1894, with Texas filling out a seven-game schedule that included matches against Texas A&M, Arkansas, and Missouri. Reginald De-Merritt Wentworth became the team's first paid coach, earning $325 for his efforts, and the former captain of Williams College built around the play of Morrison and the kicking and running of standout Ad Day.

Texas cruised through its early schedule, shutting out A&M, Tulane, the Austin YMCA twice, and then easily handling a weary Arkansas team that had taken six days to reach Austin by train. After a 57–0 rout at San Antonio, in which the game was called seven minutes into the second half at the request of the overmatched home team, the Texas squad began to entertain an invitation from Stanford to play in Los Angeles on January 1, 1895. The Texas players began freely talking about how they were going to "show the Californians how they play the game in Texas."

First they had to play Missouri at Hyde Park. Missouri jumped to a 12–0 lead and rolled to a 28–0 victory. "To say this waterloo was a sockdoliger for the backers of the Varsity boys is putting it mildly. They were dumbfounded," wrote the *Austin Daily Statesman.* Some players cut their hair to avoid being recognized as players and others, including Day, left school, never to play again. Day later recalled in a letter he had written from Alberta, Canada, where he had settled, "We were getting pretty swell-headed by the time Missouri came along and tore up our line like it wasn't there. I sneaked out of town that night and cut out my 'football course' at the University of Texas."

Football was in disarray at Texas and the team didn't get a coach to replace Wentworth until October 1895. But Frank Crawford, who had coached two seasons at Nebraska, came in and emphasized physical conditioning and playing football the way it was developed at Yale. The result was a first, and last, in Texas history—an unbeaten, untied, and unscored-upon season.

Texas fielded solid teams the next few seasons, but it wasn't until 1898 that the program took another major step.

The year before, the sport had fallen under control of the Athletic Council, a faculty committee formed in 1895. They hired David Edwards, a former Princeton player and Ohio State assistant, as head coach. Texas went 5–1, with a loss to Sewanee, and also got its first permanent home when the Athletic Council made a $1,000 down payment to buy a field just east of the Main Building. When students arrived in the fall, a fundraising effort netted another $1,460 and the purchase neared completion.

Burnt orange is perhaps the most easily distinguished color in college athletics, but the first colors the teams wore were a more vibrant orange. When the baseball team was waiting for a train to go to a game in nearby Georgetown in 1884, supporters wanted to wear something that set them apart from other fans. Students were dispatched to downtown Austin and they returned with orange and white ribbons.

Though the colors were popular, some fans wore old gold and white. Seeking to settle on one combination, the Austin and Galveston medical campuses voted in 1900. Orange and white drew 562 out of 1,111 votes, outpacing orange and maroon and royal blue.

In 1904, *Daily Texan* editor D. A. Frank lobbied successfully to have the field renamed for university proctor James B. Clark. Frank would later make a more lasting impression with another plea. In 1903, he began labeling the team "The Longhorns" in his stories and the name began to stick as a replacement for the more commonly used "Varsity" and "Steers," though it wasn't until former manager turned businessman Lutcher Stark gave the team a set of orange-and-white blankets embroidered with "Texas Longhorns" that the name stuck.

As the sport grew in the early 20th century, Texas continued winning, but a revolving door of coaches made it hard to get consistency. In 1903 the Board of Regents approved the creation of the post of athletic director, who would oversee the athletic program while coaching football, baseball, and track, and hired Ralph Hutchinson.

A year later, the Longhorns had a chance to make a national name for themselves, scheduling games at St. Louis and Chicago. Texas easily handled Washington University 23–0 in the first game, and then took a train to Chicago to play Amos Alonzo Stagg's feared Maroons.

Chicago newspaper accounts painted the Longhorns as big, bruising, and fast. The imaginative reporters talked of how carpenters had to lengthen the beds the Texas players slept in by six inches, and how a pistol range had been set up nearby so they could, as good Texans, get in their daily shootin' practice. As for their diet, the *Chicago American* wrote, "The Texans live on raw chopped beef, fresh blood from newly stuck cows, toast, fruit and milk. Each man drinks a half a pint of gore each morning for breakfast."

It made for a good story, but it didn't help the Longhorns. Texas drove deep in Chicago territory on the opening drive but then fumbled, and Maroons lineman Walter Eckersall scooped up the ball and ran 100 yards for a touchdown. The rout was on. Chicago piled on 10 more touchdowns and the ensuing 68–0 humiliation remains the most one-sided loss in Texas history.

Keeping a head coach remained a problem—Texas had 13 different coaches in its first 19 seasons—and it wasn't until Dave Allerdice arrived in 1911 that the program developed consistency. Versatile newcomer Clyde Littlefield was a native Pennsylvanian who moved to Texas when an oil find near Beaumont lured his father. Littlefield ended up earning 12 letters in basketball, track, and football and even dabbled in baseball, where he reportedly batted 1.000 before having to give up the sport because of time constraints.

Football rules were changing to emphasize the forward pass, and the strong-armed Littlefield, who could throw the ball 60 yards on the fly, opened up the Longhorn offense. Texas went 22–2 from 1912 to 1914, but again failed to make its name nationally. New Texas athletic director Theo Bellmont invited Notre Dame, which boasted an end named Knute Rockne, to come to Austin for the 1913 season finale.

Notre Dame, then known as the Ramblers, was prepared for Texas, going so far

Henry "Doc" Reeves was a legendary figure who tended to the Varsity's ailments early in the 20th century.

as to create a countermove for Paul Simmons, who, because ball carriers weren't down until they were covered up, liked to flip over opponents, get up, and keep running. The Ramblers had one man hit him low from the front, the other high from behind, to slam Simmons on his back. Notre Dame broke open an early 7–7 tie and rolled to a 30–7 victory. Despite the margin, the Longhorns were encouraged that they could play with the national powers.

College football of that period had few rules governing eligibility and even looser enforcement of them. On May 6, 1914, officials from eight schools met at the Oriental Hotel in Dallas to plan a conference that could regulate the game. Players had to establish residency for a year and then had three years of eligibility. On December 14 in Houston, the schools Arkansas, Baylor, Oklahoma, Oklahoma A&M, Southwestern, Texas, and Texas A&M became charter members of the Southwest Conference. Rice

and SMU would join in the next four years.

During the early years of the Texas program, Henry "Doc" Reeves, an African-American, joined the team as a janitor and later a trainer for the football teams. Wearing his customary vest and fedora, Reeves would answer to the call of "Water, Henry," and he lovingly cared for the bumps and bruises of the Longhorns. This was the era of segregation, however, and Reeves was the subject of racial taunts from opponents. During a game at Arkansas fans called him "Dr. Snowball," and jumped him after the game. The November 1914 alumni magazine, *The Alcalde,* described him as the "guardian angel of all athletic teams." Reeves filled the post loyally for 20 years before being felled by a stroke in 1915. He died in February 1916. Eighty-five years after his death he was selected to the Longhorns' Hall of Honor.

Allerdice's Longhorns finished the 1915 season 6–3, 2–2 in the first year of the Southwest Conference. Even though his teams had gone 33–7, and he gave the program much-needed stability, he grew weary of criticism from Texas fans and moved to Indianapolis to enter his family's meatpacking business.

Texas moved on and continued to prosper under coaches Bill Juneau and Berry Whitaker, going 9–0 and giving up only 14 points under Whitaker in 1918. When Whitaker left, the school was unable to hire a big-name coach

PAUL SIMMONS FAMOUS DIVE
TEXAS - NOTRE DAME GAME 1913

above: Notre Dame legend
Knute Rockne, far right,
watches a Ramblers kick
clear the uprights in 1913
in Austin.

left: Paul Simmons gets
pancaked in 1913 by Notre
Dame tacklers wise to his
favorite flip move.

because it could offer a salary of only $4,000. The Longhorns lured E. J. Stewart from Clemson and he did an admirable job, going 24–9–3 in four seasons, including a 3–1 mark against Texas A&M, but he would lose his job in a political struggle after the 1926 season.

Bellmont felt Stewart was too distracted by the summer camps he ran in nearby Kerrville, and replaced him with his assistant and former Longhorn great Clyde Littlefield. Though the move would ultimately be very positive for Texas, it created enough hard feelings that Bellmont lost much of his political base. He was placed on "probation" in 1927 and then on October 1, 1928, the Board of Regents voted 8–1 to reassign him to chairman of the physical education department.

Bellmont's inelegant departure came not before he made one of the lasting contributions to Texas football. In 1922 it started to become apparent that Clark Field and its wood bleachers could no longer contain the crowds the Longhorns were drawing. On Thanksgiving Day of 1923, Bellmont met with student leaders, outlining his plans for a new stadium and asking for their support. Stark vowed to match 10 percent of the funds raised, but it was students who raised the bulk of the funds through blood drives and scrimping on meals. Excavation on the new facility, to be named Memorial Stadium in honor of the dead from the recent war to end all wars, began on April 1, 1924, and the stadium was dedicated during the Longhorns' game with A&M on Thanksgiving Day.

Littlefield's first three seasons were unspectacular—6–2–1, 7–2, 5–2–2—but that changed in 1930. Though only one starter returned from the previous season, two sophomores who arrived unheralded quickly earned their places on the varsity: Harrison Stafford, whom a Houston reporter would later described as "built like a greyhound, but runs a trifle faster," and burly fullback Ernie Koy.

Stafford was given a ragged jersey and mismatched shoes on his arrival, but he quickly caught the attention of the coaches when he leveled halfback Dexter

Shelley during a scrimmage against the varsity. Koy, meanwhile, gave Littlefield the fullback he was seeking and behind two stalwart linemen both nicknamed "Ox"—guard Grover Emerson and tackle Claude Blanton—the Longhorns went 8–1–1 in 1930 and 8–2 in 1932.

The fortieth season of Texas football, in 1933, was noteworthy for something besides the anniversary. Koy, Stafford, and 14 other lettermen were gone and although Texas started the season 2–0, they were routed 26–0 at Nebraska and never seemed to recover. The Longhorns lost three of their last four games, salvaging only a season-ending 10–10 tie with Texas A&M. The Athletic Council voted unanimously to bring Littlefield back for an eighth season, but he sensed he didn't have Stark's support and instead resigned, staying on as track coach and winning 25 conference titles before he retired in 1961.

Jack Chevigny had played on Knute Rockne's first team, and was one of his favorites, as a player and an assistant. He seemed destined to replace Rockne when the legendary coach retired, but when Rockne died in a 1931 plane crash in Kansas, Notre Dame officials deemed the 25-year-old too young for the job and gave it to assistant Hunk Anderson.

Disheartened, Chevigny took a job as head coach of the NFL's Chicago Cardinals, but he longed to get back into the college game. He did so at St. Edwards, a tiny private school about five miles

above: Billy Disch, Theo Bellmont, Doc Stewart, and Clyde Littlefield shaped the face of Longhorn athletics in the 1920s and for decades to come.

below: Jack Chevigny had Knute Rockne's gift for oratory, but not his knack for winning, with the huge exception of the landmark upset of his alma mater, Notre Dame.

across the Colorado River from Texas. His first team won the Texas conference and Longhorn boosters took notice. Chevigny returned the interest, even running a down marker on the sidelines during Texas games.

When Littlefield quit, the Athletics Council plowed through a series of candidates and nominated Northwestern assistant coach Pat Hanley. Chevigny, however, through his job at St. Edwards, his magnetic personality, and his Notre Dame pedigree, had already won over the Board of Regents.

Chevigny went 7–2–1 in his first season, including a 7–6 victory at Notre Dame that finally gave the Texas program the national cachet it had long sought. After the season he was given an $800 raise and a LaSalle automobile. The good feelings, though, were not to last. His attempts to recruit from the same pool as Notre Dame proved disastrous, he alienated Texas high school coaches, and detractors grumbled that he spent too much time on his law practice. He went 4–6 and 2–6–1 in his next two years, resigning four days after the 1938 season ended with a 6–0 loss at Arkansas.

Texas had long tried to underpay coaches and had nothing but inconsistency to show for it. Grudgingly, Stark told the Board of Regents that it was time to open up the university's purse strings and get the best coach available. It was no secret who they wanted—Coach Dana Xenophon Bible.

TEXAS LONGHORNS OF 1941
AND BIG BOY THEIR MASCOT

D. X. Bible was no stranger to the Longhorns. From 1917 to 1928 he led Texas A&M to a 72–19–9 record, which included SWC titles. Lured by bigger money, he moved to Nebraska, where in eight seasons, 1929–36, he won 74.3 percent of his games and captured six Big Six titles. At both schools he was a combined 5–6–2 against the Longhorns.

He would cost Texas—at $15,000 a year his salary was almost double that of university president H. Y. Benedict— but it would be worth it. Bible immediately patched up relations with the state's high school coaches, hiring one of the best, Amarillo's Blair Cherry, as an assistant. He met with those he felt he needed to unite the program, telling them, "Gentlemen, when we leave this room, we'll all be calling the same signals."

He didn't tell them they'd have to be patient, but they soon realized that was necessary. Bible's first two teams went 2–6–1 in 1937 and 1–8 in '38, the latter salvaged by a season-ending upset of Texas A&M, which the next year would win its only national title.

Bible's huge recruiting class began to jell in 1939, and a stunning last-minute touchdown by Jack Crain on a screen pass upset Arkansas 14–13. Though the Longhorns would finish 5–4, the victory over the Razorbacks gave Texas its first win in an SWC opener since 1933 and gave Bible's program some needed momentum.

His efforts would come to fruition in 1940, when Bible's recruiting had the team stocked with talent, including a backfield of Crain, Pete Layden, and Noble Doss, and line strength in Chal

The Longhorn team of 1941 poses with its mascot, "Big Boy."

Daniel and Stan Mauldin and end Malcolm Kutner.

Texas hosted A&M, which was riding a 19-game unbeaten streak and expected to roll behind its pair of All-Americans, guard Marshall Robnett and fullback John Kimbrough. Texas came out throwing and on the fourth play of the game Layden threw deep to Doss, who made a remarkable over-the-shoulder catch to the 1-yard line. Layden scored on the next play, Crain kicked the extra point, and the Longhorn defense held, giving the Longhorns a stunning 7–0 upset.

The Longhorns had earned respect, and it was reflected in their being the heavy favorite to win the 1941 SWC title. During the first six games of the season they beat all of their opponents by at least 28 points—one more than they allowed in all six games combined. After a 34–0 rout of SMU, the Associated Press voted the Longhorns No. 1, jumping Minnesota, and *Life* magazine put the faces of fourteen Longhorns on its cover and an eight-page spread on the program inside.

Baylor didn't figure to offer much resistance, having lost its last four games, including a 48–0 defeat by A&M, but it stayed with the Longhorns and after Doss dropped a long pass for what would have been the go-ahead touchdown, the Bears hung on for a 7–7 tie. The next week TCU rallied from a 7–0 deficit to beat then No. 2 Texas and ruin all hopes for a national championship season.

"What a fiasco that was," Doss said sixty years later, still ruing his drop. "Everybody was sick as dogs. I had Baylor on my mind and TCU on the field a week later."

Still, the Rose Bowl was considering the No. 4 Longhorns to play against Oregon State, which had beaten rival Oregon 12–7 to finish its regular season. There was one sticking point—the Rose Bowl was worried the 7–1–1 Horns' Dec. 6 game against Oregon could hand them a two-loss season.

Reportedly, the Rose Bowl asked Bible to cancel the game against the Ducks. Bible told the Rose Bowl officials: "No, I won't cancel it—but I'll guarantee a victory." That wasn't good enough for the Rose Bowl folks, who went ahead and picked Duke to play Oregon State.

Instead of going to the first bowl game in school history, the Longhorns were going nowhere—and stewing mightily about it. Oregon paid for their anger. Texas went 70 yards in 10 plays for a touchdown on its first drive and poured it on. Nine Longhorns scored a total of 10 touchdowns, two safeties, and seven conversions. Blocking back Vernon "Pappy" Martin, who had seemed destined to finish his Longhorn career without a touchdown, was put in late in the game and scored.

As the clock wound down, public

Doak Walker of SMU reaches high for a pass as Tom Landry closes in for the tackle.

address announcer Potsy Allen informed the crowd, "Coach Bible won't like this, but there's a message: a telephone call from the West Coast. Does anybody want to talk?"

Texas won 71–7, but the celebration was short-lived. At 11:55 the next morning, December 7, Japanese naval aviators attacked Pearl Harbor. A restaurant on The Drag had put up a sign that read, "Texas 71, Oregon 7," but then added, "One at a time. Japan next." Four members of the '41 team would lose their lives in the service of their country.

It turned out Texas wouldn't have gotten its trip to California anyway. Government officials, concerned that the expected Japanese invasion of the West Coast could come at a time when the roads in Los Angeles were crowded with fans going to the Rose Bowl, can-

celed the game. Organizers moved to Durham, North Carolina, home of Duke, where Oregon State won 20–16. Texas, meanwhile, would have to wait 63 years to make it to Pasadena, though the delay would ultimately prove worth it.

Despite the onset of World War II and the depletion and turnover of the roster because of service in the armed forces, Bible was able to keep the Longhorns winning. It helped that Bobby Layne, who came to Texas to play baseball for legendary coach Billy Disch, was talked into giving football a try as well. Layne, a high school teammate of Doak Walker at Highland Park near Dallas, was a versatile player who became the standard by which Longhorn quarterbacks were still measured near the turn of this century.

Layne was in the Merchant Marine at the start of 1945, serving with Walker, but upon their discharge in New Orleans in September, the plan was for both to go to Texas. Layne arrived as scheduled, but Walker was talked into going to SMU by old friend Rusty Russell.

"If Russell hadn't gone to SMU that year, I'm convinced we'd have had Walker and Layne as teammates," Bible told Lou Maysel in *Here Come the Longhorns, Vol. 1.*

Having Layne was pretty good by itself. Texas was 9–1, with only a 7–6 loss to Rice, heading into the Cotton Bowl against 14-point underdog Missouri. Layne put on a one-man performance that has never been matched in the annals of Longhorn football, running the new split-T that Bible had adopted from Missouri and pummeling the Tigers with it. Layne ran for four touchdowns, passed for two, and kicked four conversions to account for every Longhorn point in a 40–27 victory.

Missouri Coach Chauncey Simpson, unable to find Layne on the field, caught him as he was getting on the bus and told him, "I never saw a better job by anybody."

Bible, though, was running out of steam. He rejected a 10-year contract extension in 1945, and marked '46 as his final season. He went out in style. In his final game, the Longhorns defeated his old school, Texas A&M, 24–7 at Memorial Stadium.

In 10 seasons, Bible won three SWC titles, more than the Longhorns had won in the first 22 years of the league combined. Though Bible was gone, his hand-picked successor, Blair Cherry, was there to carry on. As far as the Longhorns were concerned, more glory days were ahead.

3

"THE UNIVERSITY OF TEXAS CALLING"

One of the best kept-secrets among young college coaches in the mid-1950s was cloistered away in the Northwest, doing a bang-up job at Washington. It might as well have been Iceland, for as much as it showed up on the University of Texas radar when the Longhorns went looking for a new coach in 1956.

Texas, having just reassigned Ed Price after a 1–9 season, wanted a big name. Former Notre Dame Coach Frank Leahy campaigned for the job.

Darrell Royal and Arkansas Coach Frank Broyles, rivals in the Southwest Conference, flipped the coin when the teams met in 2003.

Murray Warmath of Minnesota, Stu Holcomb of Purdue, and Bill Murray of Duke were all contacted. Tommy Prothro, a great young offensive mind then at Oregon, also popped up. Texas officials compiled a long list of candidates, more than 100 by some estimations, and began culling through them. But to a man all the big names they contacted said thanks but no thanks. So Texas officials got an inspiration. Instead of getting the big name, they decided, let's talk to the big names and get their ideas on an up-and-comer.

They went to Bobby Dodd of Georgia Tech. They got back in contact with Michigan State's Duffy Daugherty. Both told them about a 32-year-old former Oklahoma All-American who learned well at the side of Bud Wilkinson and who had success wherever he went. He might suffer a little from wanderlust, but was worth examining. Even Paul "Bear" Bryant, then in his final year at Texas A&M, put in a good word, though according to *Here Come the Longhorns, Vol. I* he first protested. "I don't want you in the league whipping my pants off me," Bryant told Royal.

One night, Darrell and Edith Royal were in bed ready to go to sleep when the phone rang. On the other end was the operator. "Long distance calling," she said.

Then a man came on the phone. "This is D. X. Bible of the University of Texas."

As a boy in Hollis, Oklahoma, Royal and friends would listen to Sooners games on the radio as they played football in the front yard.

Royal cupped his hand over the phone.

"This is it, Edith," he whispered excitedly. "This is the University of Texas calling."

Though Texas didn't know much about Royal, he knew the Longhorns. He had always respected their teams. Hollis, Oklahoma, where he grew up, was just a few miles from the Red River and he spent many Friday nights playing football against Texas's best. Both his parents and sets of grandparents were from Texas. On one trip from Oklahoma to Mississippi, when he was coaching at Mississippi State, he and Edith detoured through Austin, taking a look at the campus.

Washington was a fine program and he felt comfortable there, but he couldn't shake the distance. "Our kids never got to see their grandparents," he said. "It cost too much to fly and we didn't have the time to drive. Texas was a lot closer to home and the people talked like I did. Washington was a great coaching job but I never felt like it was home."

He knew Texas's distance, its pride and, more important, its potential. As if to get a further taste of what awaited, he went to see *Giant,* the sprawling Rock Hudson and James Dean movie that explored the relationship between the old business and new money in Texas.

Royal told Bible he was interested. Within days he was on his way to Austin in what turned out to be a whirlwind courtship. Bible picked him up at the airport and whisked him to the office of university president Logan Wilson, who told him what the expectations of academic performance would be. They then went to meet with the Athletic Council. Before leaving for Austin, Royal had quickly and methodically quizzed Bible on the names and faces of all the members of the Athletic Council and the Board of Regents, from their titles to the best way to address each one of them. Royal wowed the Athletic Council and then met with regents president Tom Sealy and some of the other board members at the Commodore Perry Hotel. The university, trying to avoid the publicity that came with the contacts of Leahy, Dodd, and Daugherty, asked Royal to travel and check into the Adolphus Hotel under an assumed name. He chose that of his Washington line coach, Jim Pittman. The subterfuge was working until a man approached Royal outside president Wilson's office and put out his hand. Royal introduced himself. So did the man, who was a reporter for the Associated Press. By the time the word got out, though, Texas had a new football coach. The entire process took less than five hours.

"When I came to Texas I had no idea it would be for anything more than an interview," Royal said. "No one was more surprised than I when I walked out of the meeting with the job."

Royal took the job before settling on money. He remembers telling them he

BARBARA GENE ROBERTSON
B is for Bobby, She's often late, but boy, they say she's more fun on a date.

J. D. SIZEMORE
J is for J. D., so quiet and so shy, but get him in a crowd, and he's quite a guy.

JOYE VAUGHAN
J is for Joye, she's quite a lass, in beauty contests she leads the class.

CECIL SUMPTER
C is for Cecil, he's determined to fly, but get him in Dallas and he is already high.

DARRELL ROYAL
D is for Darrell, the pride of the school, reckon some day we'll lose him to Gould?

MILDRED IRMA POLING
M is for Midge, with eyes big and brown, as "Hyacinth Adams" she was the talk of the town.

MARY KATHERINE SMITH
M is for Mary, Boogie-Woogie is her cue, hear that change? It's Rhapsody in Blue.

Royal was an All-State player at Hollis High School and was popular with his classmates.

wanted to concentrate on coaching and not also assume the athletic director duties, and that his salary was flexible. He only asked that it be of market value. "Don't embarrass me or yourself," he told them.

Texas gave Royal a five-year contract worth $17,500, a $500 raise over what he made at Washington.

It was big money for a man from such humble beginnings. Born on July 6, 1924, he was the sixth child of Burley Ray and Katy Elizabeth Royal in tiny Hollis, Oklahoma, tucked in the southwest corner of Oklahoma near the bend in the Texas Panhandle. Royal never knew his mother, who died four months after his birth. He was never told why she died, but always assumed it was from complications of childbirth. His middle name, K—no period—comes from her name.

"The MKT railroad came through town and the kids called it the Katy," Royal recalled. "Because of my middle initial they started calling me Katy. They had no idea that was my mother's name.'

Burley Royal, who was born in Montague County, Texas, worked a variety of jobs, as a truck driver, bookkeeper, and jailer. When Katy died he moved the family in with his parents. Eventually he built a new house and remarried when Darrell was six.

Shortly after that, his sister Ruby died of food poisoning. Four years later his oldest sister, Mahota, a married mother of two, died of a heart problem.

Mahota's family moved in with the Royals, and with the country heading into the Great Depression and dust storms ravaging Oklahoma, times were tough. Darrell got a job as a paper boy and later picked cotton, filling nine-foot sacks in the arid, dusty heat.

In his free time he began to frequent Hollis High School football practices, where he studied Coach Dean Wild and the football techniques he taught. By the time he reached junior high, he was already diagramming football plays when his mind wandered from school lessons. He began to consider a career in coaching.

In the spring of 1940 Royal had just finished junior high school when Burley decided to join the exodus of Oklahomans to California. They headed to Porterville, California, where Royal's stepbrother lived, and bought a farm.

Royal immediately disliked California. He did not get along well with his stepmother and he was teased because of his Oklahoma drawl.

"It was a little bit of a show of weakness on my part, but I started working hard to keep from talking like an Okie—because they could spot you at the snap of a finger," Royal told Jimmy Banks in *The Darrell Royal Story.* "And it wasn't one of those things you could be proud of, because 'Okie' then was really a dirty word."

Royal also got a letter from Coach Wild, who was now the head coach at

Hollis High and offered to get Darrell a part-time job so he could get by while he played football.

It also didn't help that the football coach at Porterville wasn't impressed with his latest import. "He told me I had to play JV because of my weight," Royal said. "I asked, 'Can't I just try out?' He said no. He wouldn't budge."

Royal borrowed $13 from his father, packed all his belongings in a hollowed-out Victrola case he used as a suitcase, and set out to hitchhike back home.

When he arrived he moved back in with his grandmother, got a job working for a car dealer, and set out to play football. Because he had moved away, however, he didn't meet the necessary residency requirement.

"I was born in Hollis, had gone to school every day of my life but the state board declared me ineligible because my dad had moved," Royal said.

When he regained his eligibility, Royal's running, passing, and punting prowess earned him first-team All-State honors and some recruiting interest, but when he graduated in 1943 he said good-bye to his family and the girl he'd been dating for a year—Edith Thomason—and joined the Army Air Force.

Trained as a tail gunner, he was assigned to a B-24 crew and sent to Arizona for heavy bombardment training. Just as the training was about to be completed, his crew was selected out of the 60 on base to be reassigned to photo reconnaissance at what is now Will Rogers Airport in Oklahoma City. Days before being shipped out, his crew was picked to specialize in weather reconnaissance.

When that training was done they received orders to report to Guam, but Royal developed appendicitis and had emergency surgery. While he recovered, his crew shipped out. At the time, Royal said, the Air Force wasn't forming new crews, so he was in limbo, spending some time shooting baskets at the base gymnasium. There he was discovered by a captain who recruited him to the base basketball team. Eventually, he was invited to join the Third Air Force football team at Drew Field near Tampa, Florida.

There he played for Tennessee alumnus James Quinn Decker, running the triple wing alongside some former college and even professional players,

including Charley Trippi and Bob Kennedy.

Royal, who had married Edith on July 26, 1944, shortly after her high school graduation, and was the new father of a baby daughter, was discharged in late 1945 and turned his sights on playing college football. His reputation as a player had grown by his exploits in service ball and he received a variety of scholarship offers, but he opted to go with the team he followed as a child on his transistor radio, the home-state Sooners.

There he rapidly became an all-around star, first as an ace defensive back, punter, and return man. After three seasons as backup quarterback, he took over the Sooners' split-T in 1949 and led the Sooners to an 11–0 record that was capped with a 35–0 Sugar Bowl rout of LSU, giving the Sooners the momentum needed to win their first national title the following season. His exploits earned him some All-America mentions, but his mark on the OU record book is indelible. He still owns the OU records for career interceptions (18) and longest punt return (96 yards).

Royal's backfield coach was Bud Wilkinson, who would later build a dynasty at Oklahoma in the 1950s, and Royal would say no other coach had a

bigger influence on his future coaching style.

"More than any other coach, by far," Royal said. "The way he taught quarterbacks, the private sessions, the philosophies. He's an excellent teacher. He had intended to be an English teacher. He was good at teaching the fundamental football that to him was not that complicated. People saw there's a great football player who doesn't know the system. I suggest changing the system and play the great player. That's what Bud Wilkinson would have done."

Royal began his coaching career in charge of the freshman backfield at North Carolina State, where he helped Coach Beattie Feathers switch to the split-T. A job offer from Tulsa allowed him to move closer to home, but it came at a cost. While he was en route to Tulsa, new Oklahoma Coach Bud Wilkinson was trying to reach him about a spot on the Sooners' staff but, unable to contact him, filled the spot.

A better job as backfield coach under Murray Warmath lured him to Mississippi State in 1952. A former teammate, Claude Arnold, was playing for the Edmonton Eskimos in the Canadian Football League and when the Eskimos went looking for a new coach in 1953, Arnold suggested Royal. He had never seen a CFL game, knew nothing about 12-man football, but it was a head coaching job and the Eskimos were offering $13,500, money he never thought he'd see when

he was shining shoes in Hollis. He took the job.

Royal's high-mileage ride on the coaching carousel was far from done. A year later he was back at Mississippi State, this time as head coach replacing Warmath, who moved to Minnesota. This time Royal stayed two years, both 6–4 seasons, with the highlight being a 12–7 victory over Alabama in 1954, the Bulldogs' first victory over the Crimson Tide in 13 years.

Up at Washington, the Huskies were trying to recover after firing John Cherberg amid allegations of player payoffs. Intrigued by the size of the school, its budget, and its large following, Royal jumped at the chance and moved his family, which now included three children, to Seattle. His only team went 4–4 and placed fourth in the Pacific Coast Conference, but it overcame quarterback injuries and finished strongly, with victories over Stanford and Washington State.

Then Texas called. The task facing Royal wasn't an easy one. When Bible had retired as coach in 1946, the program seemed to have a good foundation. Blair Cherry, a former high school coach and Bible's right-hand man, succeeded him. Gruff and simple, he was a football-first coach who had little use for the media, fans, or alumni.

Cherry switched to the T-formation in 1947 and went 10–1 behind Bobby Layne, who was quickly becoming one of the best quarterbacks in college football. The No. 3 Longhorns met No. 8 SMU before 45,000 in Dallas in a showdown for the Southwest Conference title, a game that also featured the final showdown between Layne and his former high school teammate, Doak Walker. The teams were tied 7–7 when Gil Johnson hit Walker on a 54-yard pass in front of Longhorn defender and future Dallas Cowboy coach Tom Landry, who finally dragged Walker down at the 1. Dick McKissick scored from there, but Layne hit Byron Gillory for a 14-yard touchdown to bring the Longhorns back, although their bid to tie the score failed when Frank Guess's kick went wide left. Late in the game, with the Longhorns driving, Layne turned to hand off to Landry on a key fourth-down play, but Landry had slipped and the play went nowhere. SMU ruined the Longhorns' hopes for an unbeaten season, 14–13.

Cherry's team, though highly competitive, never approached that level again and midway through the 1950 season, with his team at No. 5 in the country, rumors began circulating that Cherry's ill health—he suffered from insomnia and ulcers that he would later attribute to "overemphasis on winning"—would force him out. Cherry initially refused to confirm the reports, but on the Wednesday before the Baylor game he verified them, saying he would retire on December 31 to go into private business.

Texas decided to go a proven route, and elevated Cherry's line coach and onetime aspiring sportswriter, Ed Price, to the top job. Price, like Cherry a bright football mind who lived football, had run the Longhorn defense and promised to be a capable successor. With stars like Bud McFadin, Gib Dawson, and Carlton Massey, his second team won the SWC title outright and the next one shared it. Expectations were high for the 1954 squad, but it lost to Notre Dame 21–0 in the second game and struggled home at 5–4, the Longhorns' first losing season since 1938.

Price revised his coaching staff and

Royal and wife Edith pose with their children at the door of the airplane that brought them to Austin in late 1956.

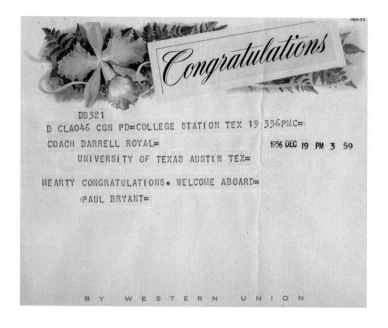

Texas A&M Coach Paul "Bear" Bryant welcomed Royal. A year later Bryant left the Aggies for Alabama.

Mike Campbell, far right, was a brilliant football mind who molded some of college football's stingiest defenses.

bled his recruiting efforts and produced a strong class, but it wasn't enough to save him. The Longhorns, with only four players left from a senior class that was 41 strong when it got to Texas, didn't have a single player named to the All-SWC team, the first time that had happened since 1935. Midway through the season, which ended with a 1–9 mark, worst in school history, Price resigned.

After being named coach, Royal couldn't wait to get started. He packed the family car in such a hurry they left Edith's suitcase at home. Royal had also promised his children, Marion, eleven, Mack, nine, and David, four, they'd stop at Disneyland on the way to Texas, and he made good on the vow, although he had to speed to make up time. He got caught.

"I handed the patrolman my driver's

his offense, moving from the split-T to the "belly series," but despite a strong sophomore class that featured halfback Walter Fondren, the Longhorns went 5–5. Desperate to survive, Price redou-

license and he wrote out the ticket," Royal told Banks in *The Darrell Royal Story.* "Then, as he handed it to me, he said, 'Well, Mr. Royal, if you can get that Texas football team to run as fast as you drive, you'll do all right.'"

What Royal inherited, though, was closer to a Model T than a Thunderbird. The facilities were antiquated and dirty. The assistant coaches shared one small locker room. The field was covered with weeds and burrs. Royal's own office was an eight-by-eight room tucked in a corner at Gregory Gym. He didn't even have a secretary.

Royal persevered. He took a no-nonsense approach and demanded discipline, erecting a tower from which he could watch all facets of practice. He had a talented quarterback in Walter Fondren and several other talented sophomores from Price's last recruiting class. The 6–4–1 record was better than could be expected one year removed from the worst season in school history, and there were wins over Arkansas and Texas A&M, but the season ended on a down note in the Sugar Bowl. Royal, very familiar with Mississippi from his days at rival Mississippi State, instituted two-a-day practices but the move backfired, and his team was embarrassed 39–7 by the Rebels.

Over the next 19 seasons Royal would know many triumphs. His teams would go 167–47–5 and win seven SWC titles outright and share four more. He would

win national titles in 1963 and '69 and share one in 1970. His teams would reach the No. 1 ranking in seven different seasons.

Even as Royal was winning his second national championship, he was taking steps to do what critics had hoped he would have done much earlier—integrate the University of Texas football team.

Texas had made history of a dubious sort in 1946 when an African-American, Herman W. Sweatt, applied to the Texas

above: Royal sits in his modest office at Gregory Gym. After being rewarded with an honorary teaching title Royal sat in his chair and joked that he didn't know how many f's were in professor.

below: Dapper and calm, Royal walks the Texas sideline at Memorial Stadium early in his career.

Law School but was denied admission. The university tried to dodge the problem by creating all-black Texas State College for Negroes, which would later become Texas Southern, but the U.S. Supreme Court ordered that the law school accept Sweatt. But progress was slow and eight years later the school had yet to accept a black undergrad.

Even though there were rules against blacks competing in Memorial Stadium, in 1954 Washington State halfback Duke Washington became the first to play there, and his 73-yard touchdown run in a 40–14 Texas victory opened some eyes.

Two years later the Board of Regents voted to admit black undergrads. That

fall Southern Cal fullback C. R. Roberts ran for 251 yards in a rout of Texas at Memorial Stadium, but still there was no movement in football.

Shortly after Royal arrived his team was involved in an ugly racial incident in the 1960 Cotton Bowl game with Syracuse. A brawl erupted near the end of the first half, which reportedly started when a Texas player disputed a referee's call and then told a black Syracuse player who tried to intervene, "Just keep your black ass out of it." The incident made national news and Royal requested an NCAA investigation to clear Texas's name, but none was forthcoming.

Meanwhile, the Board of Regents was dragging its feet. In 1962 the body addressed athletic integration by announcing that it would do nothing "which would disturb the excellent relations existing between the University of Texas" and the other SWC schools.

Royal tried to get things started in 1963, contacting Bubba Smith of Beaumont, but he couldn't promise Smith he'd be eligible, so Smith went to Michigan State, where he was an All-American end. The Board of Regents had turned over its membership, and with more progressive members such as Wales Madden and Frank Erwin, the regents announced on November 9, 1963, that extracurricular activities, including athletics, were now open to all students.

It hardly started a rush. The following spring James Means of Austin made the

John Harvey of Austin Anderson High School became the second black player to sign with Texas. Royal then signed the cast on Harvey's leg, the result of a basketball injury.

track team as a sprinter and became the first black in SWC history to letter in any sport.

The following spring Royal tried to recruit San Antonio's Warren McVea but, according to Richard Pennington's comprehensive book on the integration of the Southwest Conference *Breaking the Ice,* the Longhorns backed off because they learned of a police record and questionable work habits, not the combination needed for someone who had to be strong enough to be a pioneer.

In 1966, SMU signed Jerry LeVias, who did as much to enlighten the rest of the conference by leading the Mustangs to their first Cotton Bowl in 18 years as by his signing. Texas pursued Mike Williams of El Paso in 1967 but he didn't have the grades.

One of the Longhorns' most ballyhooed recruiting classes, the famed "Worster Bunch" that formed the core of a team that won 30 consecutive games and two national championships, arrived on campus in 1967 amid growing student protests and pressures to integrate. Almost lost in the hype was the more quiet arrival of a pair of black walk-ons, E. A. Curry and Robinson Parsons. A year later the Longhorns signed their first black recruit, Leon O'Neal of Killeen, and although O'Neal had the courage to weather the storm, he wasn't up to the task academically and was forced to transfer out.

Before he left, O'Neal helped recruit

Tackle Julius Whittier of San Antonio, who would go on to be a Dallas lawyer, in 1970 became the first black football player to letter.

a pair of black athletes to sign with Texas in February 1969—John Harvey of Austin Anderson and Julius Whittier of San Antonio Breckenridge. Royal signed Harvey for a front-page photo in the *Austin Statesman,* after which he also signed the cast on the leg Harvey had broken playing basketball. Whittier's signing drew less coverage. Neither article in their respective hometown papers mentioned the significance of their race.

Harvey didn't make the grade academically, instead heading off to Texas-Arlington, where he had a solid career, leaving Whittier, a powerful lineman, to play on the Longhorn freshman team as the varsity became the last all-white national champions in 1969.

Even as Whittier became the first black to letter in football at Texas the following season and the Longhorns shared the national title, a scandal grew out of comments that were attributed to Royal at a college football convention in Washington, D.C. An Associated Press story quoted Royal as telling several

black coaches, including black college coaching legend Jake Gaither of Florida A&M, that black coaches "weren't scientific" enough to coach in all-star games.

An angry Royal called the writer, Bob Greene, and told him he wasn't even at the convention, but at the Texas football banquet at the time. Greene conceded he got the information secondhand and the AP printed an apology and even Gaither came out in support of Royal, but the damage was done. Years later black athletes being recruited by Texas would be told that story and another that had Royal boasting he could still win the SWC without black players, a quote that has never been substantiated.

"There's no doubt that racism was a smudge, a stain, on the image of the university," Whittier said. "The unwillingness to accept black people for so long was a smudge, but the change was inevitable. If I had to do it all over again, I would do the same thing. Going to Texas was a great experience for me."

And for Texas. As an undergrad Whittier wrote editorials on minority recruitment for *The Daily Texan* school newspaper, and earned a philosophy degree in 1974 and later a master's degree from the LBJ School of Public Affairs and a Juris Doctor degree from the Texas Law School. He is now in private practice in Dallas.

By the early 1970s the Longhorns were beginning to bring in black talent. Roosevelt Leaks arrived and starred in 1972, the same year the Associated Press did a five-part series on racism in Texas football that examined tokenism, racism, and the lack of a social life for blacks. Still, the Longhorns were able to bring in some of the state's top black talent in the mid '70s, including Earl Campbell, Alfred Jackson, Johnny "Lam" Jones, and Johnnie Johnson.

The Longhorns had just begun shedding the image of "the man" among blacks in the state, but they had a ways to go.

Royal told Banks in 1973 that he had become weary of explaining his stance on race relations. "I'm just tired of trying to defend it," he said. "I'm just going to go by my record and my deeds and my thoughts and, eventually, the record is going to be tallied up. I'm going to do what I think is right and do the very best job I can, and in the end, I think it will be tallied up right."

Recognizing that moment might be a long time in coming, he added, "But in the meantime I guess I'm just not going to be able to convince people that I don't beat my wife and I don't kick blacks."

Royal, too, was starting to wear down from other pressures. After a dip to 8–3 in 1971, he had the Longhorns back to 10–1 in '72, 8–3 in '73, 8–4 in '74 and, with an out-of-this-world sophomore fullback named Earl Campbell in '75, back up to 10–2. And there was one specter that haunted all those seasons—a loss to Oklahoma, a school he had

facing page: Texas's 17–13 win over Alabama in the 1973 Cotton Bowl allowed Royal to hold a 3–0–1 edge against Bryant in head-to-head meetings.

grown to despise because of its alleged cheating and spying.

In 1973 his daughter Marian Royal Kazan died as the result of an automobile-bus collision. Sadly, he would lose a son, David, in a motorcycle accident in March 1982.

Royal said his daughter's death didn't have anything to do with his retirement, but as he told John Wheat in the oral history *Coach Royal,* "it softens your approach. Makes you understand that some things are not as important as you thought they were. It made me look at what I was doing in the game and the intensity and that maybe—maybe—it wasn't all that important. I think I eased back and became a little softer and not quite as aggressive after that as a coach."

His 1976 team gave promise the OU streak might end, but Campbell pulled his hamstring in spring practice and again in the fall and was never able to be a consistent weapon. Discouraged by changes in recruiting, which he saw turning into a lawless free-for-all, and by the changing scrutiny and pressures of the profession, Royal decided to retire.

His old coaching rival and buddy,

Frank Broyles, had announced earlier that the December 4 game in Austin would be his last. When asked if he was considering quitting in the week leading up to the game, Royal protested weakly. Hours before kickoff against the Razorbacks, a specially called meeting of the Athletic Council was convened and Royal submitted his resignation.

Campbell, his hamstring finally sound, ran for 131 yards and two touchdowns and the Longhorns beat Arkansas 29–12 to keep Royal from having his first losing season at Texas.

Royal went on to spend another three years as athletic director and then served as a special assistant to the university president, a post he still holds at 82. In the spring of 2006, he recalled the feelings he had over lunch at Barton Creek Club. The emotion of the moment was still obvious.

"I was tired," Royal said, and you can feel it in his voice. "I felt like it was time. I didn't want to stay until people wanted me to leave. It was time to set the bucket down."

Texas would spend more than two decades trying in vain to find the right man to pick it up.

4

THIS IS
OUR YEAR

The call for a reunion went out in early 2000, a celebration of the team that persevered and won the University of Texas's first national championship. They were to meet in Houston for a weekend of golf and conviviality, to catch up and tell stories.

The guest list, however, didn't stop with the members of the 1963 national championship team. Also invited were members of the 1961 and 1962 teams, whose roles in that championship season

were as undeniable as those of the Duke Carlisles and Tommy Fords.

"The fact that we didn't finish what we started propelled them," said Pat Culpepper, a linebacker on those squads. "A lot of guys from the '63 team said we showed the way. We got close. You have to get close sometimes before you can win it."

And they got close. Agonizingly close.

Ask many of the national championship players about their place in history, and they'll quickly tell you they weren't the best of the bunch in the early 1960s. They'll point to the 1961 team, with halfbacks James Saxton and Jack Collins, fullback Ray Poage, tackle Don Talbert, end Bob Moses, quarterback Mike Cotten, and linebackers Johnny Treadwell and Culpepper.

"I've said before, there's no question that was our best team," said David McWilliams, a center-defensive tackle and captain of the 1963 team. "The reason we won it in '63 was because '61 set the tone. When we were behind A&M in the second half in '63, it kept coming up that 'We're not going to let it happen again.'"

The 1961 Longhorns were built around the desire to have Saxton—a speedy back who at first frustrated coaches with his east-west running before he learned to turn it up in the hole—get the ball as much as possible. To that end, Coach Darrell Royal implemented the flip-flop offense, which put Saxton at halfback and simplified many of the blocking schemes, which cut down on play busts.

The line was young and the Longhorns would have to rely heavily on a sophomore class, but the Associated Press still made them No. 4 in the country. Royal shook his head at the lofty ranking and drawled, "That's as strong as Sadie's breath."

The new offense showed sparks in a 28–3 opening game victory over Cal, but really took hold in a 42–14 rout of Texas Tech with a 35-point first half in which the average scoring drive was less than six plays. Oklahoma had already dropped games to Notre Dame and Iowa State when the teams met in Dallas, but an impressive 28–7 win moved the Longhorns up to No. 3.

There they stayed for three more weeks until they went to SMU, where on the way to the game one of their buses was hit by a car. The car driver, bleeding, was taken to a hospital and the

Halfback Phil Harris tries to get outside the Navy defense in the Cotton Bowl victory that made the Longhorns unbeaten national champions in 1963.

players crammed on the other bus to get to the game.

Shaken, they played SMU to a scoreless first half, but then Saxton broke an 80-yard touchdown run early in the second half and the Longhorns pulled away to win 27–0.

Texas survived its collision that day, but Michigan State and Mississippi weren't so lucky. The Spartans were shocked 13–0 at Minnesota and the Rebels lost 10–7 at night to LSU in Baton Rouge. Texas was now No. 1 in the Associated Press and United Press International polls, only the third time the Longhorns had ever been atop the AP poll and the first time since a one-week stay in 1946.

A week after crushing Baylor the Longhorns hosted TCU. The Horned Frogs were a 25-point underdog and everything seemed fine with the world as the Longhorns went through their final walk-through on Friday at Memorial Stadium, but then a norther blowing sleet moved in that night, bringing a stark shift in the winds of fortune with it.

Royal knew what TCU was capable of doing. In 1959 the Longhorns were 8–0 going into their game with the Frogs on another cold day that was so raw that Bevo the mascot steer quickly retreated back into his trailer. The Longhorns wasted a 9–0 lead and a backup halfback named Harry Moreland broke a 56-yard touchdown midway through the fourth quarter to hand the Long-

horns a 14–9 loss. In one of his memorable lines, Royal said of the Frogs while trying to explain the loss of opportunity, "They're like a bunch of cockroaches. It's not what they eat and tote off, it's what they fall into and mess up that hurts."

That was a statement the Frogs would not soon forget, and when they came to Austin in '61 they came loaded with bluster. TCU quarterback Sonny Gibbs guaranteed a victory and went deep early, but Carlisle intercepted. As Saxton was running a sweep he was tripped, did a somersault, and took a knee to the head. The resulting concussion sent him to the bench with fullback Ray Poage already hurt, and the Frogs made a key fourth-down stop.

Tommy Ford running behind two-way line standout Scott Appleton was a sight feared by Longhorn opponents.

It boiled down to one play, when Gibbs got the ball back on a reverse and heaved the ball 50 yards to Buddy Iles for the game's only touchdown in a 6–0 Texas loss.

"Looking at the movies afterward, I don't think we ever played a worse game," Treadwell said. "TCU was higher than a kite and that ball bounced funny because it's shaped funny."

"We had something that was in our reach, something that was for all time," Royal told the media after the game. "That balloon has popped. If we win Thursday [against Texas A&M], we can still get in the top ten, and when it's all melted down, that's not so dusty."

Forty-three years later you can still hear the wistfulness in Royal's voice when he talks about that game.

"That day TCU upset us they crossed the 50-yard line one time," Royal said, not counting the Iles touchdown. "The odds of somebody winning that kind of game if they're anything close in personnel—that was an unusual upset."

Texas crushed A&M 25–0 and earned a spot in the Cotton Bowl against Mississippi, which had tormented Royal during his days as a coach at Mississippi State and in his first season at Texas. After the 12–7 victory, his players carried him from the field.

The 1962 season held as much promise, but it began on a tragic note that stunned Royal to his core. In August, during one of the hottest summers in recent history, fourth-string freshman guard Reggie Grob and two other Longhorns collapsed from heat exhaustion during workouts and were taken to the hospital. The other two players recovered, but Grob's body temperature soared and he was placed in a refrigerated suit. Royal coached the team during the day and stayed with Grob at night but tests soon revealed Grob had irreversible kidney and liver damage. He

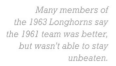
Many members of the 1963 Longhorns say the 1961 team was better, but wasn't able to stay unbeaten.

was taken to a Dallas hospital for more treatment, but eighteen days after he had collapsed, Grob died.

Royal began doing some serious soul searching. "All those things go through your mind," he said. "If we hadn't run wind sprints. If we hadn't done this or done that. If we hadn't been practicing football."

Grob's parents wrote Royal a letter thanking him for all he'd done for their son. That helped Royal see another side.

"You get back to thinking realistically and take the percentages and see the good that's done. You think about quitting it, but then you start thinking about driving cars, thinking about the people hurt driving cars. Do you quit? No matter what you quit, you can't stop the process—the process of life."

The conventional wisdom of the time was that withholding water during workouts toughened players. Now the Longhorns had regularly scheduled water breaks and their performance during the hottest workouts was closely monitored.

Though the Longhorns had lost most of their offensive punch, they still had a stout defense that would hold six opponents to six points or less. They began the season ranked No. 2, but after a 9–6 win over Oklahoma and a less than inspiring 17–7 win over Vanderbilt by No. 1 Alabama, they moved into the top spot.

They were determined to stay there

this time, and a famous goal-line stop by Treadwell and Culpepper and a fourth-quarter touchdown drive helped them come from behind to edge Arkansas 7–3.

Next up was Rice. The Owls were coming off a 15–7 upset loss to SMU, but Royal was wary. "We haven't licked them down there since I've been at Texas," he said. "I'm not chesty about going down there. I just hope we can scratch one out one way or the other."

They couldn't. The game turned into a close-to-the-vest affair, but the Longhorns appeared to take control when Ford's 55-yard punt return set up a 9-yard touchdown run by Jerry Cook, but Rice came back to tie the score at 14–14 at halftime. Twice in the second half the Longhorns punted instead of going for it on fourth-and-1 near midfield and a final drive stalled inside the Rice 40 with less than a minute. The Owls ran out the clock.

Stunned by the criticism that erupted in the wake of the tie, which dropped the Longhorns to No. 5, Royal considered banning local writer Lou Maysel from practice. He sought counsel from Governor Allan Shivers, who according to Royal biographer Jimmy Banks told him, "When you're in a position as prominent as you are and have to deal with the press all the time, there's no way you can win a running battle with the press."

Royal understood and it eventually led to one his more famous quips:

"Never argue with someone who buys his ink by the barrel."

The Longhorns, though, faced more important matters than any quarrel with the press. David McWilliams can still remember the empty feeling he had as he sat on the steps of the Longhorns' dorm with Scott Appleton and Tommy Ford after the '61 loss to TCU. When the trio became captains, they inherited what had become a summer tradition. Every couple of weeks, one of them would write a postcard to every player. Usually the cards were filled with inspirational sayings, reminders to stay in shape, eat right, and behave, but this time they ended almost every card with the same thought.

"This is our year," McWilliams remembered writing. "We've been at the top for two years and we've let it slip away. We just can't do it this year."

Royal, never one to dwell on negatives as reinforcement, chose another approach.

"If you talk about losing, don't do this, don't do that, you can get so paralyzed you can't move," Royal said. "I always tried to use stuff that would cause them to be aggressive."

Sports Illustrated and Street & Smith picked the Longhorns No. 1, but eight starters were gone, including the heart of the defense, Culpepper and Treadwell. There was also uncertainty at quarterback. A three-way rotation in '62 between John Genung, Duke Carlisle, and Tommy Wade kept the offense from coming together, and Royal vowed he would not repeat that.

Genung had graduated, leaving Wade and Carlisle to battle it out. Wade was the better passer, but Carlisle was better at limiting bad plays. When Jim Hudson

Ford and fellow captains Appleton and David McWilliams wrote summer postcards to teammates to avoid the disappointments of '61 and '62.

showed he could replace Carlisle at safety, the full-time move to offense was made. Elements of the Oklahoma split-T offense were added to take advantage of the speed of sophomore halfback Phil Harris.

Defensively, the Longhorns knew they'd be fine. The year before, a red-headed freshman from San Antonio tore up the varsity in scrimmages and was projected to be every bit as good as Culpepper or Treadwell. Tommy Nobis would go on to become the school's first consensus two-time all-American and the first-round pick of the 1966 NFL draft, by the Atlanta Falcons, but now he was a more-than-capable 190-pound sophomore linebacker who seemed never to miss when he aimed his face mask at a ballcarrier's belt.

Texas began the season ranked No. 5, but each week they crept up a spot until they headed into their annual meeting with Oklahoma in Dallas on October 12 ranked No. 2. Two weeks earlier the Sooners traveled west to play top-ranked USC. Los Angeles was blanketed by a record heat wave that had temperatures soaring past 100 degrees and USC Coach John McKay had suggested to Sooners Coach Bud Wilkinson that the game be moved to an evening kickoff. Oklahoma refused, and in a national television game that turned into a duel between Sooners halfback Joe Don Looney and Trojans stars Pete Beathard and half-back Mike Garrett, the Sooners won 17–12 to move into the No. 1 spot.

The Longhorns, who would go on to beat Oklahoma State that night, were watching.

"We saw most of it on TV," Carlisle said. "It was an impressive win. It was good for them to beat the defending national champion. It was also a little scary how good they looked doing it."

If Texas was going to stop Oklahoma and Looney, it would need another top-notch game plan from defensive coordinator Mike Campbell, who had quickly emerged as Royal's top assistant coach. A former B-24 bomber pilot who flew fifty missions in Europe during World War II, including the daring low-level bombing of the Ploesti oil fields in Romania in 1943 that severely crippled the Nazis' fuel production, he dissected games from the press box and was known for his rapid, and uncannily effective, defensive adjustments.

Campbell was quick with a smile and a joke, though many of his players didn't learn of that until their playing days were through.

"Did he have a wit?" Treadwell said. "I didn't know. I was scared to death of him. I didn't want him to look my way."

Treadwell and the others knew, however, that when Campbell had something to say you listened.

"We won a lot of games with Mike Campbell," Treadwell said. "He was just a football genius. He knew what 22 people were doing every play. Every play. Can you imagine that? We won so many games just because of him."

Oklahoma had built its attack around the hard running of halfback Looney, who when he chose to play, was nearly unstoppable. Today's multiple offenses mean that teams game-plan now more against schemes and formations than personnel, but McWilliams said the edict back then was simple—stop Looney.

"Mike Campbell's theory was that you've always got to make them beat you left-handed," McWilliams said. "You take away what they do best. He'd say that if someone keeps hitting me on this side of the head, I believe I'll turn my head."

That's what the Longhorns did. Looney drew a crowd wherever he went, and the Longhorns stifled him on the opening drive and then moved the ball with ease, jumping to a quick 21–0 lead.

"That set the tone," McWilliams said of the score on the opening drive. "We've got them. We can move the ball. Now we just have to stop Looney."

Looney gained only six yards and conceded afterward, "We were just too cocky." It was his last game as a Sooner. Wilkinson, fed up with Looney's erratic behavior, which included a fistfight with a student assistant coach the week before, booted his star halfback from the team.

Now the Longhorns were in familiar territory—No. 1—with a familiar but until then impossible prospect—keeping it.

"That put a lot of pressure on us," McWilliams said. "It sounds stupid, because that's where we wanted to be, but it was, 'Okay, we're there but we're still six games away. And we've got Arkansas up next.'"

Texas jumped to a 17–0 lead, but the Razorbacks started coming back. McWilliams said he suspects Arkansas figured out their defensive signal for what had been an effective blitz, which wasn't complicated. When Longhorns' assistant coach Charlie Shira wanted to call 60 Pop, where the two linebackers rush, he clapped his hands.

Arkansas began taking advantage, hitting the tight end on a quick pass every time the stunt was called, McWilliams remembered. In the fourth quarter Shira called the stunt again, but this time McWilliams, playing defensive tackle in a six-man front, decided he would forgo his normal assignment and hold up the tight end.

"I'm not going," McWilliams told end Timmy Doerr.

"You've got to," Doerr said.

"Naw, they got us on that. I'm going to hold up the tight end," McWilliams said.

The ball was snapped and McWilliams engaged the tight end. "I was holding him, really," he conceded. The Razor-

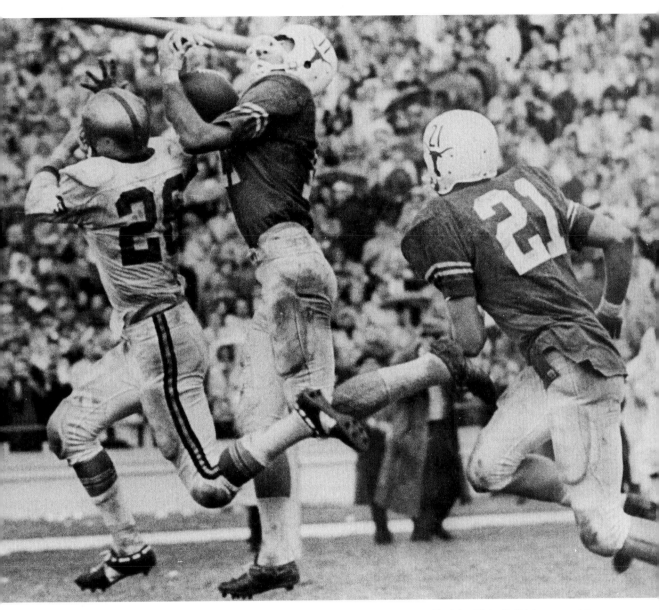

The tale of Duke Carlisle's game-saving interception against Baylor has grown to legendary proportions over the years.

backs' play failed and the drive stalled. Arkansas was forced to punt and the Longhorns held on for a 17–13 victory.

The close call was too much for Royal and his coaches. "I think we got a little cocky. The next week we got chewed out pretty good," McWilliams said.

The Longhorns edged their next two foes, Rice and SMU, by less than a touchdown each, and then faced Baylor. The Bears were picked sixth in the preseason SWC poll, but behind the pass-catch combination of quarterback Don Trull and receiver Lawrence Elkins, they had opened league play with four straight wins.

It had all the makings of a game that would humble the Longhorns. "That's the reason coaches can't jump up and say, 'We're the cock of the walk and we will play anybody,'" Royal said.

Neither team managed much offense early, but the Longhorns pulled ahead 7–0 early in the third quarter. Tommy Ford converted on fourth-and-3 from the Baylor 4-yard line and set up a touchdown plunge by Tom Stockton. Meanwhile, the Bears' Trull-Elkins combination couldn't click.

"We controlled the ball, kept them off the field and used up the clock," Carlisle said. "Mike Campbell said the most beautiful sight to him all game was when he looked over to the Baylor sideline and saw Don Trull warming up because he had been out of the game so long."

Stockton's touchdown appeared to be enough to stand up, particularly after Hix Green intercepted a Trull pass and Carlisle scrambled for a first down with 2 minutes, 14 seconds left.

Line coach Jim Pittman turned to Royal. "It's in the bag," he beamed.

Stockton fumbled on the next play and Baylor recovered deep in its own territory. Carlisle turned to jog off with the offense but didn't see Hudson coming out to relieve him. Campbell had decided, on a gut feeling, to go with Carlisle at safety, even though he hadn't played defense all season.

Trull moved the Bears downfield on short passes, getting to the Longhorn 19 with 29 seconds left. Elkins then set up halfback Joe Dixon with an outside move and broke toward the post.

Carlisle was assigned to cover the tight end, but the Longhorns' eight-man rush had him occupied. He looked over at Trull.

"I knew because of our rush that he had to throw where he looked first, which was to Elkins breaking to the middle. He was looking over my shoulder so I took off."

Just as the ball appeared to settle into Elkins's outstretched arm, Carlisle sliced in behind him and made the game-saving interception, though at first he didn't think so.

"I looked down and saw the white line. I thought I'd come down at the 1," he said. "Instead of thinking we had just won the game, now the quarterback in me is thinking, 'I'm going to have to take a snap from the 1 before this thing ends.'"

What Carlisle saw was the end line. He took a knee just inside the 20 on the next play and the game was over.

Carlisle finds his part in the legend of that game amusing. "That story, as I get older, is that I was in only one play, that it was the last game of the season, and there was only one second left," he said.

There was one game left, against A&M, and it was shaping up to be a beauty. The Longhorns had twelve days to prepare but much of their thoughts during the first week of practice were about what was to happen that Friday, when they were to present an auto-graphed ball "From the No. 1 team in the country" to President John F. Kennedy.

Kennedy was a big football fan, so Royal was invited to be part of the dele-gation that welcomed Kennedy after his flight from Dallas that afternoon. "I'd been told that President Kennedy knew the Hook 'em Horns," Royal said, "and I was going to greet him as he got off Air Force One."

Royal was home, getting dressed to head to the airport and later attend a re-ception at the Governor's Mansion and a dinner at Municipal Coliseum.

"I had my tie in my hand, hadn't tied it yet when they came on TV and said the president had been shot in Dallas," Royal recalled. "I just stopped dressing then and stayed on top of the news until Walter Cronkite said the president was dead."

Texas's season was saved when officials ruled Jim Willenborg of A&M didn't have possession of this late interception before he landed out of bounds.

*Carlisle's sneak on a muddy field in College Station
gave the Longhorns a 15–13 victory and
their first national title.*

Beating the Aggies and winning a national title became the furthest thing from the Longhorns' minds.

"That night in the dorms we were talking about conspiracies, about going to war," McWilliams recalled. "What's going to happen? We had just lived through the Bay of Pigs, so we had no idea. That was the first time I saw sincere concern over something other than football, grades, or girls."

School officials considered postponing or canceling the game, but it went on as scheduled on Thanksgiving Day in College Station.

A&M Coach Hank Foldberg called on the memory of the Longhorns' upset of the defending national champion Aggies in 1940. "I would like to see us avenge that defeat that hurt so much," he said. Foldberg had another dedication in mind. Two days before the game the president of the Aggie Club, Ben Templeton Jr., and his wife were killed in a plane crash in Louisiana. Shortly before halftime of the game, with A&M up 7–3, television cameras caught Foldberg giving Templeton's mother a message. "Mrs. Templeton, we'll win this one for Ben."

The Aggies had more than emotion going for them. When the Longhorns arrived at Kyle Field they found a surface bare of grass and ankle-deep in mud that had been painted green.

"We were told A&M had practiced on the field and chewed it up, so they

put fresh dirt on it and then it had rained," Ford remembered. "It was a quagmire. It was like running in quicksand. You were just slipping and sliding around out there. You were fortunate if you hung on to the ball."

Royal, clearly incensed, said before the game, "This is a disgrace. There is a lot riding on this game and our boys deserve the chance to show what they can do."

Frank Erwin, a regent who had not yet reached the peak of his power as the body's chairman, wanted to force the Aggies to forfeit. "Regardless of which

69

THIS IS OUR YEAR

Texas Governor John Connally tried to watch the A&M game from his hospital bed in Dallas but the excitement proved to be too much.

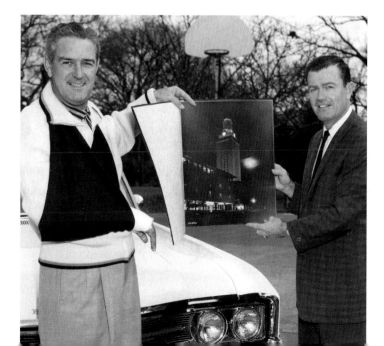

team eventually wins today, the condition of the playing field is a disgrace and a reflection upon A&M and its athletic department," Erwin said.

A&M President Earl Rudder apologized, but pointed out that someone had tried to burn the word "Bevo" into the field and that no doubt contributed to its condition.

The field didn't seem to slow the Aggies, who got two long touchdown passes from Jim Keller, the second a 29-yarder to George Hargett in the third period that put A&M up 13–3.

Ford scored on a 2-yard run early in the fourth quarter but the Longhorns missed the two-point conversion. When the ensuing Aggie drive stalled, Bobby Lee tried a 42-yard field goal that fell short. Texas took over at its own 20 with 5:28 left to play.

Wade hit Hix Green with a swing pass that gained 20 yards and passed to end Charley Talbert for another 10. He tried to go back to Talbert on a short pass but Aggie end John Brotherton stepped in for an easy interception. Instead of falling down, Brotherton tried to lateral and Tom Stockton recovered for Texas at the Aggie 45.

"If he had just fallen down," Royal recalled, "the game would have been over."

Four plays later Wade went for it all, looking deep for George Sauer. The ball soared over the head of Sauer and into the outstretched hands of a diving Jim Willenborg. The officials ruled he didn't have possession as he crossed the end line.

"That was the greatest injustice on a group of young fellows I've ever seen," Foldberg said. "Our Aggies were No. 1 today. We played them right off their feet."

Willenborg's disputed interception has taken on a life of its own. Carlisle recalled meeting one of the game officials at a gathering a few years ago. "He introduced himself to me and said, 'I have to tell you, he was out. We both ruled that and weren't even looking at each other.' I told him I really appreciated that. Then I introduced him to an A&M guy I knew and he told him the same thing. After the official walked away, the Aggie said, 'I don't know. That guy seems a little addled.'"

Carlisle scored on a 1-yard quarterback sneak with 1:19 remaining and the Longhorns escaped with a 15–13 victory and their first national championship.

From his bed at Parkland Hospital in Dallas, where he was recovering from gunshot wounds, Governor John Connally watched the game, and his wife, Nellie, called the A&M coach's office. Royal was summoned to the phone to hear Nellie pass along his congratulations. "Nellie said the governor got so excited she finally had to turn the TV off," Royal said to his team after the call. "I told her sometimes I wished I could have turned things off, too."

The team dedicated the game to

Connally and sent him the football they had all autographed for Kennedy.

Austin reveled in the Longhorns' first national championship, and offered a revealing peek at the growing Longhorn sense of expectation and entitlement. Friday morning the *Austin American* carried a full-page ad that read, "Congratulations to the National Champions." The ad was placed by the American National Bank. The deadline for the ad was the day before the game.

For his part, Royal didn't even want to consider who was waiting in the Cotton Bowl. "I'm going to do my damnedest not to even think about football for a few days," he said. "All the rooters of the Orange and White have a lot to be thankful for, athletically speaking."

Although the bowl game would have no bearing on the AP and UPI titles, which then were announced at the end of the regular season, the Longhorns didn't want to leave any doubts.

The Cotton Bowl gave them that opportunity against No. 2 Navy, whose coach, Wayne Hardin, had done plenty of politicking for his Midshipmen to be ranked No. 1. He had the help of the Eastern media, which looked at the Longhorns with disdain. Myron Cope, who would later gain fame as the inventor of the "Terrible Towel" that Pittsburgh Steelers fans waved during their Super Bowl runs of the 1970s, was particularly derisive.

"Tune in your television to the Cotton Bowl and you'll laugh yourself silly," Cope wrote. "Texas is the biggest fraud ever perpetrated on the football public."

In preparing for the game, Royal and his staff made two key observations. First, the Navy defensive signals were, ironically for a military academy, very

Dared to pass by a Navy defense loaded up against the run, Carlisle had a record-setting day in his duel with Roger Staubach.

easy to decipher. Secondly, if they were to beat the Middies they would have to contain the scrambling and broken-play ability of quarterback Roger Staubach.

To contain Staubach, Campbell devised a drill that would emphasize the pursuit angles necessary to contain Staubach, who was a master at reversing field and buying time.

"The defensive coaches told us every time Staubach got outside containment he had thrown a touchdown pass," McWilliams said. "He was phenomenal. You could be coming at him from behind on a dead run and somehow he'd spin out of it. We used it as conditioning and it would go for three or four minutes. We had to keep contain and tighten contain. If you were on the backside, your job was to get behind

Royal doesn't remember Tommy Nobis ever missing a tackle.

him and get a yard deeper than him, so when he spun he'd come right at you."

Five days before the game, Virginia McWilliams, David's mother, was felled by a stroke. Virginia had high blood pressure and as a Christmas present to her son had agreed to get a physical. An appointment was set for January 10.

McWilliams flew to Cleburne on the private plane of alumnus Johnny Holmes and rushed to the hospital. "I got there at 5 P.M.," McWilliams recalled. "She died at six."

Royal told his captain, 'You playing in this game is a personal decision. It's up to you to decide if you're going to play.'"

McWilliams's father, Dennis, told him Virginia would have wanted him to play.

"Yes sir," David told his father. "I think my mother has the best seat in the house."

Staubuch sent McWilliams a telegram with his condolences. When they met at midfield on January 1, 1964, for the coin flip, McWilliams thanked him.

By that time the Longhorns were possessed. "We almost killed each other running onto the field," McWilliams said.

The final spur had come courtesy of the pregame interviews CBS conducted with the coaches at midfield before kickoff.

Hardin went first and gave a small speech, wrapping up with "when the

*Phil Harris turned a short gain into
the Longhorns' first touchdown against Navy.*

Ford was a 5'7" battering ram, of whom Royal quipped, "He'd be a six-footer if he hadn't played football."

challenger meets the champion and the challenger wins, there's a new champion."

Royal, biting his lip, uttered two words. "We're ready."

"I thought it was a great pep talk," Royal said of Hardin's remarks. "I wanted to hug him."

Ford felt it. "Normally a coach says one or two sentences but he went on and on," Ford said of Hardin. "It just got everyone teed off. He probably did as much getting us ready to play as anything."

Texas didn't go into the game expecting to fill the air with passes, but they had little choice but to take the invitation of Navy's 5-4-2 defense. "They jammed up on us so that we had to," Royal said. "Their corner linebackers were closer to the line of scrimmage than

we had seen in the films. It was like a picket fence."

Less then three minutes into the game Carlisle threw a flare to Harris in the right flat for a 58-yard touchdown. In the second quarter he threw a 68-yarder to Harris.

Meanwhile, the Longhorns' preparation paid off as Staubach could not get loose. He completed 21 of 31 passes, both Cotton Bowl records, but his only touchdown came on a two-yard run after Texas had already built a 28–0 lead.

"I thought I could run, I thought I could throw, but I've never been knocked down harder than I was today," Staubach said after the game. "Texas must have really had us scouted. I just got knocked on my tail, and that's all there is to it."

Hardin, whose team failed to back up

his bold talk, was gracious in defeat. "I've never seen a team that deserved to be No. 1 more than Texas," he said.

Rear Admiral Charles C. Kirkpatrick, superintendent of the Naval Academy and a native Texan from San Angelo, came into the locker room to congratulate Royal, telling him, "You rascal, you beat us at our own game."

Texas had thrown for 234 yards and Carlisle set a Cotton Bowl record for total yardage, with 267 by the time he was removed in the third quarter.

"One of my teammates came up to me and said, 'Thank God Staubach set the Cotton Bowl passing record. It would have been strange if you had held it, Carlisle,'" he remembered.

Carlisle is now in the oil business in McComb, Mississippi, but his phone is ringing more than it ever has. The 1963 Longhorns went where no other Texas team had gone, and people still want to talk about it.

"Somebody said, 'Carlisle, you're getting more publicity now than you did when you played,'" Carlisle said. "He's right. There's interest now in what hap-

pened to the old guys who won the first national championship. When we won the Rose Bowl, people talked about '63, '69 and '70. We got to celebrate that more, along with the new one."

Thousands of Longhorn fans came to Robert Mueller Municipal Airport to see Phil Harris and the Cotton Bowl victors.

5

"YOU'RE NOT GOING TO BELIEVE THIS"

James Street is blessed. He knows he is. He can't avoid it.

His place in history is secure as the quarterback of what had been the Longhorns' last unbeaten national championship team. He is routinely included in the discussions of the best quarterbacks in Texas football not because he was the most gifted thrower or the fastest runner or the

James Street gets the fourth-down call from Darrell Royal that set up the winning touchdown to beat Notre Dame.

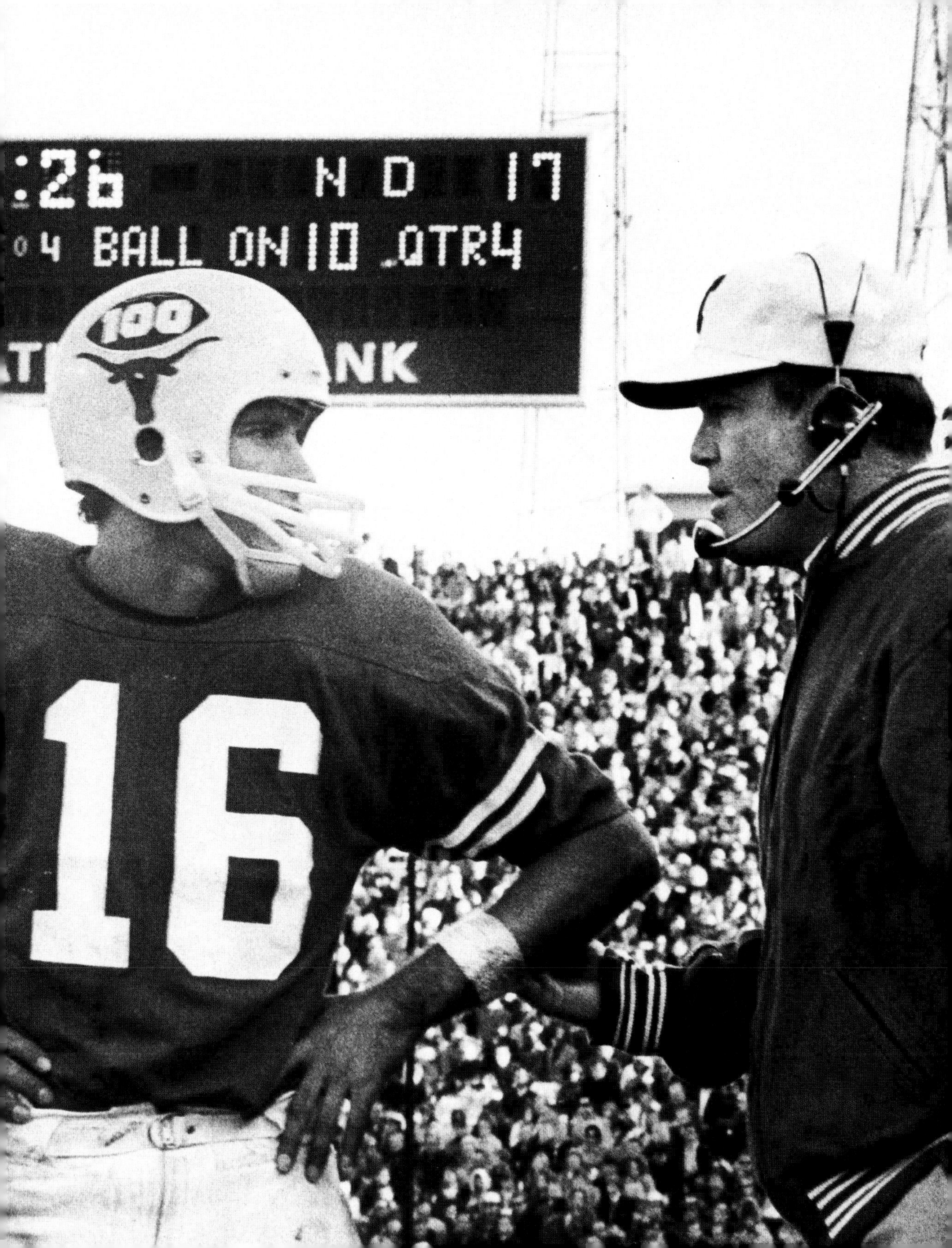
:26 N D 17
4 BALL ON 10 QTR4
NK
100
16

most prolific rusher or passer. James Street just never lost.

"I realized how lucky we are," Street said. "We had two or three things that could have gone either way, but they went our way and we won. So, consequently, 35 years later I'm talking to you."

Nineteen hundred and sixty-nine was a pivotal and turbulent year in the world. Richard Nixon was inaugurated as president amid the escalation of the Vietnam War. James Earl Ray pled guilty to killing Martin Luther King and Sirhan Sirhan was convicted of murdering Robert Kennedy. Yasser Arafat became president of the Palestine Liberation Organization. The Boeing 747 and the Concorde had their maiden flights. Neil Armstrong became the first man to walk on the moon. The U.S. Supreme Court ordered the end of all segregation. *Sesame Street* debuted. Music fans invaded a farm in upstate New York for the Woodstock Music Festival. Reports of the massacre of Vietnamese civilians at My Lai began to surface. Followers of Charles Manson murdered actress Sharon Tate and six others.

And Texas won the football national championship.

The road to the 1969 title was filled with success and landmark change, with close calls and legendary exploits. It marked the high point of an era and, in a strange way, the beginning of the end

of one of the greatest runs in Texas history.

Though the Longhorns lost a talented group from the '63 champions, a list of all but three starters that included Outland Trophy winner Scott Appleton and All-SWC halfback Tommy Ford, they returned the one man who made the most difference. Oklahoma Coach Bud Wilkinson retired after the '63 season, and the Sooners made some overtures to Royal, but after a brief flirtation he decided to stay.

To reward him, the Board of Regents boosted his salary from $20,000 to $24,000 and, in a move that angered many of the faculty whose careers depended on getting tenure, awarded him a full professorship.

Royal tried to make light of the situation by saying the promotion left him perplexed. "I've been sitting here in my office for 30 minutes trying to figure out if professor has one *f* or two *f*s in it."

Texas had a strong linebacking corps in Timmy Doerr and Tommy Nobis and a deep and versatile offensive backfield that included fullbacks Harold Philipp and Tom Stockton, wingback Phil Harris, and Ernie Koy, who could play either halfback or fullback. Jim Hudson, who moved to safety the season before, when Duke Carlisle took over the quarterback duties, moved back and nailed down the starting job.

After shutout wins in their first two games, the Longhorns were back to No.

1 in the AP poll. Decisive wins over Army and Oklahoma followed and the Longhorns headed to Arkansas with momentum but also with a long injury list. Hudson was back at practice but he still hadn't fully recovered from sprained knee ligaments in the second game against Texas Tech; ends George Sauer and Knox Nunnally and tackle John Elliott were nursing bad shoulders.

Arkansas took advantage of the Longhorn injuries when Ken Hatfield found a breakdown in the Longhorns' punt coverage and the nation's leading punt returner took it back 81 yards for a 7–0 second quarter lead. The Longhorns tied it early in the fourth quarter when Phil Harris scored from the 2 on fourth down.

Two costly Texas mistakes led to Arkansas regaining the lead. An illegal substitution call wiped out a Razorbacks punt and when Joe Dixon bit on an outside route, Bobby Crockett ran past him for a 34-yard touchdown and a 14–7 lead.

Much like the '62 game in Fayetteville, when the Longhorns drove late for the score, they moved 70 yards and scored on a short Koy dive with 1:27 left. Royal called timeout, talked it over with his coaches, and decided to go for a two-point conversion and the win. Marvin Kristynik's pass to Green came up just short.

"We'd lost to Arkansas or we would have been back-to-back champions," Nobis said. "We knew we were knocked out of a shot at the national championship, but it was still a major bowl and we could still end up with a great Texas season."

"YOU'RE NOT GOING TO BELIEVE THIS"

Street, Jim Bertelsen, Steve Worster, and Ted Koy formed a strong backfield, but the offensive line was a question mark heading into the '69 season.

Arkansas won the rest of its games but even the upset of the No. 1 Longhorns wasn't enough to sway the UPI or AP voters, who gave their title to Alabama. The Orange Bowl, eager to pit the old national title against the new one, set up a Texas-Alabama matchup that was sealed when the Tide beat Auburn 21–14 on Thanksgiving Day.

"We wanted to show people we were as good as anybody," Nobis said. "That was our national championship."

And Royal was at his motivational best. Pat Culpepper, then an assistant, remembers how Royal handled the buildup. "That thing had been built up so much. They'd come in with all this Bryant propaganda from the press. We came back from pregame warm-ups. Coach had such neat handwriting. He wrote up there, 'Nobody lives as much as we do—Paul Bryant.' And he walked away. A few minutes later the officials come and say 'let's go.' Coach Royal walked back up to the board and wrote, 'B.S.—DKR.' Then he said, 'Let's go prove it.'"

Alabama quarterback Joe Namath had a bum knee and it was uncertain if he'd play. After warm-ups, he was cleared to play but Coach Paul Bryant held him out. Texas was able to contain his replacement, Steve Sloan, and was leading 14–0 when Bryant decided to put in his star.

Namath quickly passed Alabama to a touchdown and the Longhorns coun-tered on a short plunge by Koy with 23 seconds left in the half. Alabama scored 10 unanswered points to open the second half and when Kristynik threw a ball up for grabs Alabama intercepted at the Longhorn 34.

Two completions gave Alabama a first down at the 6 and then fullback Steve Bowman carried to the 2. Bryant decided he wasn't going to get fancy, and sent Bowman into the line on two carries that netted only a yard.

"That was pure Bear Bryant football," Nobis said. "When you get down to it, his philosophy was if we deserve to win the game, then we can punch it in on four downs, our guys against their guys."

On fourth down, Namath tried to sneak in over right guard. Tackle Frank Bedrick hit him first, and then Nobis squared up on him. The whistle blew and Namath was short, but he twisted out of Nobis's grasp and crawled across the goal line.

Nobis joked, "I don't think the official was from Texas, but he could have been."

Still, he said the call was just. "He was over when he finished crawling, but when you're down, you're down. You can't crawl in," Nobis said. "He argued that night and I can see him right now. To me he looked like a combat infantry-man crawling on his belly."

Later, when Nobis was with the Atlanta Falcons, he lived in the same apartment complex as Bill Mathis, who had been a teammate of Namath's with the Jets. When Namath would visit they'd argue good-naturedly about the play, Namath insisting he scored and Nobis just as certain he didn't.

"He understands," Nobis said. "Does he accept it? Hell no, I wouldn't accept it either. But he knows that's football."

Texas had gotten within a failed 2-point conversion against Arkansas of winning back-to-back titles, but it would be a while before the Longhorns seriously challenged again. A rare three-game losing streak doomed the 1965 season to a 6–4 finish and they ended the season unranked for the first time since 1960. The next two seasons also ended with four losses and they cracked the national rankings only once, when they began the 1967 season at No. 5 and then opened with losses to Southern Cal and Texas Tech.

Royal blames himself for the dip, saying he enjoyed some of the perks of the '63 title too much instead of going back to work.

"I made some bad choices with my time," Royal said. "I went to banquets, accepting honors instead of recruiting. That didn't show up until '66 and '67, but we missed a whole solid class."

The Longhorn offense, too, had stagnated. Royal was always looking for ways to innovate. His team ran the split-T his first season, moved to the wing-T in 1959 and then the flip-flop wing-T in 1961 before settling on the I-formation in 1966. At the end of the 1967 season he shuffled his staff, moving the man he had hired the year before to coach freshman linebackers to oversee the offensive backfield instead.

Emory Bellard had long been thinking about new ways to get the fullback involved in a triple-option. Practice had already wrapped in the spring of 1968 and the Longhorns had gone back to

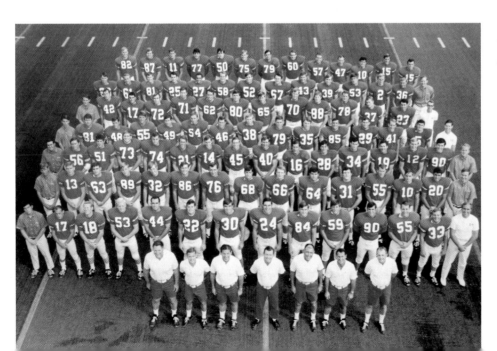

The 1969 Longhorns were the last nonintegrated team to win a national championship.

running the wing-T, but Bellard wasn't satisfied. Always armed with a pencil box and sheaves of graph paper, he doodled ideas combining the split-T, the veer, the wing-T and I-formation.

One evening he got his two sons and some of their friends and went to a local field to bring the drawings to life. Bellard played quarterback. He remembered getting two things out of the experience.

A broken finger.

And the understanding that the idea could work.

"It was very feasible, very clear it would be successful if it was operated right," Bellard recalled.

Bellard then detailed the offense in written form and made a presentation to Royal, whose interest was piqued. With former player Andy White at quarterback and several players who had just completed their eligibility filling out the backfield, Bellard demonstrated the offense for Royal at Memorial Stadium.

"I saw how it worked on the blackboard," Royal said. "I wasn't sure if we could get it taught. Emory set his jaw— 'We'll get it taught.'"

They gave the Longhorns a crash course during the '68 preseason but it was slow to take. Texas had a strong group of halfbacks, including Ted Koy, Chris Gilbert, and Billy Dale, and also the prototypical wishbone fullback in a sophomore out of Bridge City named Steve Worster.

Royal's concern was the offensive line, which was not only rebuilding but also adapting from a scrambling blocking style to a more power-oriented approach. "I don't think we're gonna jump out and average 300 yards a game," Royal cautioned. "We're just not that strong on the line of scrimmage."

The No. 4 Longhorns opened by tying No. 11 Houston and then dropped a 31–22 game at Texas Tech. Texas was using various names for the offense, from the Y-formation to simply "left" and "right." *Houston Post* sportswriter Mickey Herskowitz, noting that the formation resembled an inverted chicken pulleybone that people superstitiously pull apart to make a wish, suggested "wishbone." It stuck.

Bill Bradley came to Texas with the reputation as a do-everything player, but he just wasn't the right man to run the wishbone in games.

"There was never anyone who could run it as well as he could mechanically," Bellard said. "Bill had the misfortune of coming to the University of Texas with such fanfare, with the nickname 'Super Bill' and everything, and had the misfortune of playing on some average teams. He could punt with either foot, pass with either hand. He could catch spiral punts with one hand, just reach out and pluck it. Bill tried so hard to fulfill those expectations, I think he was guilty of trying to do too much."

The coaches also suspected that instead of reading the option, Bradley was guessing. In the third quarter of the Tech game, with the Longhorns trailing 28–6, Royal turned to Bradley's backup. "You take it on the next series," he said to Street, who led the Longhorns to two touchdowns but missed connections on a pitchout that Tech recovered to end any hopes of a comeback.

Recalled Street, "I remember him telling me I couldn't do any worse. Now that's confidence."

The team was now Street's to run, though Royal didn't make any official announcement of the change to lessen the pressure on Street and Bradley. Royal moved Bradley to split end and then to safety, where he truly excelled, paving the way to a nine-year professional career that saw him earn All-Pro honors three times with the Philadelphia Eagles.

Koy recalled: "Bill stood up in a meeting and, using Street's nickname, said, 'The Rat's going to lead us, we're going to stand behind him.' I respect him to this day for doing that."

The Longhorns didn't even blink. "You didn't think and philosophize," Koy said. "You did your part, because if you didn't somebody else could. Coach Royal could have said, '[tackle] Bob McKay's going to be the quarterback,' and we'd be ready to do our part."

Street, though, was the perfect personality to handle the high-risk, high-reward nature of the triple option, where the correct read on a pitch could lead to a long touchdown run—or a disastrous fumble.

His competitiveness was legendary. One day he was in a golf match with receiver Cotton Speyrer when Speyrer needed to hole out from 120 yards to halve the hole. Speyrer bent over to pick up the ball.

"If you don't want me to hit you over the head with my 2-iron, you'll play it out," Street told him. "It might go in the hole."

As a quarterback, he was famous for his pep talks—sometimes getting so wrapped up in selling the play that he'd announce the snap count and break the huddle without giving the play call. He knew he needed to constantly ride tackle Bob McKay and take the blame whenever he missed connections with Speyrer.

Street also earned respect with his give-and-take with Royal. "Street could push the envelope a little more than the rest of us," Koy said. "First he'd make sure Coach Royal was in a good mood and then he'd mock him."

Royal was impressed at the way Street could joke when it was time to joke and be all business when it was time to play football.

"James was a chatterbox and he'd BS around, but in the seconds before snapping the football, when it got down to the meat of the thing, it was no-nonsense," Royal said.

With Street in command of the wishbone, the Longhorns started rolling.

Nicknamed "Slick" and "Rat," the quick-thinking Street got the wishbone rolling when he replaced Bill Bradley early in the '68 season.

They won their next eight games, including double-digit wins over No. 9 Arkansas and No. 13 Southern Methodist, never failing to score at least 35 points over the last seven.

Tennessee finally appeared ready to give the wishbone a stern test in the Cotton Bowl, with the Volunteers allowing only 93.3 yards rushing a game. Street loosened up the Vols with play-action, throwing touchdown passes of 78 and 79 yards to Speyrer, and then ran the option to near perfection, keeping, handing off, and pitching for 279 yards rushing.

"I had holes to run through that were so big I couldn't believe it," Worster said. "Those Tennessee guys acted like they didn't know what they were doing."

Royal wasn't about to let the momentum go to waste. After stumbling through the '67 season, Royal tightened team rules, including curfews and standards for dress and grooming. The infamous early morning Medina Sessions, a series of calisthenics run by trainer Frank Medina and involving jump ropes and medicine balls and other implements presumed to be of medieval origin, drove that point home. That approach continued in the spring of '69.

Texas had finished second in the nation in rushing and sixth in total offense in 1968, but Royal wasn't certain the wishbone could match those totals the next season. Gone was halfback Chris Gilbert and guards Danny Abbott and Ken Gidney from offense and tackle Loyd Wainscott, linebacker Corby Robertson, and defensive backs Billy Bradley and Ronnie Ehrig. Deryl Comer was slow coming back from knee surgery and two defensive backs who were expected to join Freddie Steinmark in the lineup—Danny Lester and Tom Campbell—were changing positions, from split end and linebacker respectively.

"I think it's wishful thinking to think we could pick right up and be the same type of offensive team we were last season," Royal told reporters.

There were capable replacements, though they just needed seasoning. The Longhorn staff was particularly excited about a speedy sophomore halfback named Jim Bertelsen from Hudson, Wisconsin, who had fallen in love with the image of state. Bertelsen was a laconic sort—Spreyer once said it took 30 minutes after meeting him until he figured out Bertelsen wasn't a mute—who had a wry sense of humor. During one game the Longhorns were leading big and he was heading for a touchdown when he inexplicably dropped the ball, after which he immediately crumpled to the ground. A concerned Street rushed up, expecting the worst, only to hear Bertelsen whisper, "How's the crowd taking it?"

Besides the influx of talent, Royal had something else going for him. Though opponents had an off-season to prepare for the wishbone, no one had figured it out the season before, and with the core of a solid defense returning, momentum was on the Longhorns' side.

"We've got the swagger back in our walk and that means a lot," he said. "You know what I mean by that, don't you? That 9-1-1 last year just kind of helps you. You take a salesman who'd made nine straight sales and he feels pretty good when he goes after the tenth one. It's not cockiness, it's confidence."

The Longhorns mirrored their quarterback, right down to their occasional zaniness to keep things loose. Linebacker Glen Halsell was reputed, among other things, to have gone to class with a dead bird pinned to his shirt, bitten the head off a frog, and responded to a date's request that he drop her off at the door of her dormitory by pulling his car up the building's front steps. Speyrer liked to hit tee shots down the dorm hallway. McKay's uncanny ability to find activities to occupy his teammates earned him the unofficial title of "recreational director."

Still, there was a tinge of uncertainty when the Longhorns opened the season.

"We were coming off a tremendous year and had to replace a lot of great football players," Koy said. "Can we do that? You bang around in the spring and bang around in the fall and you still don't know if you'll have a good team. It wasn't a remarkable game. I can't even remember the score. But after that I knew we had what it would take."

No one could stop the Longhorn wishbone. The Longhorns won their next eight, and only Oklahoma could come within 10 points of the Longhorns. Oklahoma coach Chuck Fairbanks loaded up on stopping the option; Street burned the Sooners for 215 yards passing in a 27–17 victory.

In March 1969, ABC sports publicist Carroll "Beano" Cook had been looking for a game to move to early December to showcase college football's hundredth season. Defending champion Ohio State was the clear No. 1 and traditionally ended its season with Michigan, but the Wolverines entered the season unranked and Cook felt that Minnesota would upset the Buckeyes anyway.

Among those Cook talked with was Bud Wilkinson, then ABC's top color

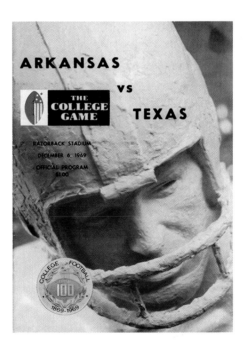

ABC television executives moved the game from midseason to December because they figured the Razorbacks would be in the national title hunt.

commentator and also a special adviser to President Nixon. Wilkinson thought the Texas-Arkansas game on October 18 would certainly be for the SWC title and perhaps for more if it was moved.

Cook's projections had Arkansas meeting Penn State in the Cotton Bowl for the national title, and he saw the move of the Texas-Arkansas games as a natural penultimate appetizer. He advised ABC executive Roone Arledge to try to move the game between the AP preseason No. 2, Arkansas, and No. 4, Texas.

Arledge left a message for Arkansas Coach Frank Broyles and he called back as he was heading to a speaking engagement. Arledge made his pitch, telling him Wilkinson thought it would be a battle of unbeatens and suggesting if it lived up to its billing, Nixon, a huge football fan, might be able to attend. Broyles, intrigued, called Royal, who approved. If nothing else, Royal felt, at least it would break up the formidable challenge of having to play Oklahoma

Despite a reputation as a poor catch-up offense, the Longhorn's wishbone attack proved resilient in come-from-behind victories against Arkansas and Notre Dame.

and the Razorbacks within eight days.

Arkansas started out whipping Oklahoma State 39–0 and Tulsa 55–0, but after the latter the AP voters leapfrogged Texas ahead of Arkansas into the No. 2 spot behind Ohio State. There they stayed as December 9 neared.

Cook's foresight was proving accurate, but there was still one obstacle. Ohio State had easily handled Minnesota, 34–7, and didn't appear to be in danger when it faced No. 12 Michigan in Ann Arbor on November 22. The Longhorns, with an open date before playing A&M on Thanksgiving, were paying attention when the Wolverines and Buckeyes met, praying for an upset.

They got it. Michigan won 24–12.

"The week of the A&M game it was all about Texas being No. 1," Koy said. "I had grown up watching that rivalry and I remembered the '63 game and how Texas almost lost. All week I didn't know if we were ready. Everybody was talking about being No. 1 and about playing Arkansas, and we've got A&M next. I remember being on the bus in front of Moore-Hill [dorm] and I didn't know if the team was ready."

The Longhorns already knew what beating Texas at home meant. Two years earlier after a 10–7 win, the Aggies left the scoreboard burning throughout the winter.

Koy, a captain, felt obligated to do something, but he didn't know what button to push. Then it pushed for him.

Stunned Razorback fans found the final score hard to believe after Texas rallied from a 14–0 fourth-quarter deficit in Fayetteville.

"We were out on the field doing our pregame warm-up, doing team drills, when the Aggie Band starts playing. 'Hullabaloo, Caneck! Caneck!' It was like a switch flipped on. Everybody got a stern, steely look. I knew we had it."

Texas rolled 49–12 and the hype commenced. "It makes them look wiser than a tree full of owls," Royal said of ABC's prescient move.

Four days before the game rumors of Nixon's visit became fact, and that he would attend with a party that would also include the Reverend Billy Graham and a young Texas U.S. representative name George H. Bush. On Wednesday, 25,000 people turned out for a pep rally at Memorial Stadium. A hog-calling contest was held and a proclamation from Governor Preston Smith was read. Royal made a few perfunctory remarks and conveyed messages from notable Texans, including anchorman Walter Cronkite, astronaut Alan Bean, and actor Fess Parker. A telegram from heart transplant pioneer Dr. Denton Cooley, another Longhorn alumnus, was relayed to the crowd: "Win or lose, I'm with you with all my hearts."

Street, as usual, was unaffected. During the week he had downplayed the challenge of playing in Fayetteville, much to the chagrin of Royal, who recalled the description once offered by defensive coordinator Mike Campbell. "Playing in Fayetteville is like parachuting into Russia."

After watching game films of Arkansas, Street remained unmoved. "We're gonna kill 'em, Coach." On the bus ride to the game, Royal sat next to Street and started telling him what two-point conversion play they would use in the game. Street listened, but knew it wouldn't be necessary.

Even as Arkansas's Bill McClard kicked off into the misty 38-degree sky, the five presidential helicopters were touching down on the practice field south of Razorback Stadium. Nixon's

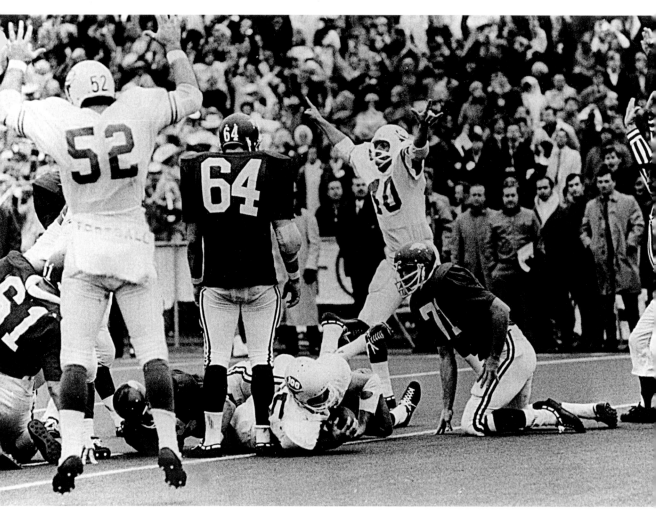

Bertelsen's touchdown tied the score and Happy Feller's point after won the national title for the Longhorns.

party hadn't even departed the helicopters and the noise level peaked again, this time when Koy fumbled on the second play of the game. Six plays later Bill Burnett scored on a 2-yard run. Street's expectations of an easy game were gone.

In the first half Arkansas quarterback Bill Montgomery threw a 26-yard touchdown pass to Chuck Dicus, but the play was wiped out by an illegal downfield block. In the third quarter, though, the pair hooked up again, and this time it counted for a 29-yard touchdown that made it 14–0.

Texas was stymied. The Arkansas eight-man front, designed to keep the option from getting outside, had been effective, holding them to no runs of longer than eight yards and forcing and recovering four fumbles. When Street tried to pass, the overstretched secondary managed to make plays, intercepting two of his passes.

Arkansas's aggressiveness, though, had planted a seed. In the first half Royal had quizzed tight end Randy Peschel on why he had missed a block on the Razorback halfback on an option to his side. Peschel said the halfback was coming up too fast to block.

"Then nobody is covering you on the pass?" Royal asked.

"Yes sir, that's right," Peschel said. Royal filed away the response.

For the longest time it didn't look like it would matter. Early in the fourth quarter, facing second and 9 at the Arkansas 42, Street couldn't find a receiver and was forced to scramble. The Razorbacks' containment broke down and Street took off toward the left corner, bouncing off a tackler at the 35 and beating linebacker Mike Boschetti to the corner of the end zone. Texas was back in the game, trailing 14–6.

Knowing they'd need a two-point conversion to win, Royal gave Street the same call they had talked about on the bus to the game, a counter option. Again, Arkansas forced it inside, but Street was able to cut up and dive across the goal line to cut the Arkansas lead to 14–8.

Just as quickly as it came, the momentum was lost. Halfback Freddie Steinmark, who clearly was having trouble running, grabbed Dicus as he sped past him and was called for defensive holding, giving the Razorbacks a first and goal at the Texas 9.

The Razorbacks went for the quick kill, but Montgomery was forced to scramble for 2 yards on first down and his elbow was hit as he passed on second down, and the ball fell incomplete. Conventional wisdom called for a run into the middle to set up McClard with a chip shot that would make a two-score game. Arkansas offensive coordinator Don Breaux called a rollout pass to the left, with Montgomery trying to hit Dicus on a quick out.

Halfback Danny Lester gave Dicus the outside, but Montgomery's off-balance pass hung, and Lester picked it off a yard into the end zone. Texas was still alive, but the Longhorns couldn't stop living dangerously. Street fumbled. The Razorbacks recovered on their own 38 but were forced to punt.

The clock read 5:51. Texas had the ball at its own 36. Three plays netted seven yards.

Royal, recalling his first-half conversation with Peschel, called "Right 53 Veer Pass," an all-or-nothing deep ball to the tight end. Street got the call and headed to the huddle, only to return for confirmation. Royal was certain.

On the sideline defensive coordinator Mike Campbell yelled, "Defense, get ready."

Street ducked into the huddle. "You're not going to believe this," he told his teammates. Then he looked at split end Cotton Speyrer and said, "Randy, I'm talking to you." If Arkansas

was peering into the huddle looking for tips, he didn't want to give them any more of an advantage. He called the play.

Peschel faked a block and went deep. Cornerback Jerry Moore took a step forward and then doubled back to run with Peschel. Safety Dennis Berner raced over. Street threw. He thought he had overthrown it.

The pass was perfect. Peschel caught it just over Moore's outstretched hands and fell to the ground at the Arkansas 13. Before the Razorbacks could recover, Koy carried 11 yards to the 2, where Bertelsen sliced over for the touchdown. Happy Feller's kick put the Longhorns up 15-14 with 3:58 left.

Arkansas moved to the Texas 38, just outside of McClard's range, but Tom Campbell tore the ball away from John Rees at the Texas 20.

Nixon presented the Longhorns with the national championship plaque,

President Nixon congratulated the Longhorns after the Arkansas victory, calling it "one of the greatest games of all times."

telling them, "The fact that you won a tough game and the fact that you didn't lose your cool and didn't quit makes you a deserving No. 1." AP and UPI, who then chose their champions following the regular season, would soon follow suit.

The Longhorn victory belonged to the team. In 1969 Texas didn't have a player lead any SWC offensive category. The Longhorns had only one consensus all-American, tackle Bob McKay, and didn't have a player finish in the top ten of the Heisman voting.

"They give me a lot of credit for that game, but if Danny Lester didn't pick off that pass before we scored and if Tom Campbell didn't get that interception at the end we wouldn't have won," Street said. "People forget about that. Like I tell people, it's not hard to win—it's hard to get into position to win."

Twenty-five years later the teams gathered for a reunion when the Longhorns visited Fayetteville for the second of a home-and-home miniseries.

"Bill Burnett, their tailback, told me at the reunion that the Arkansas players appreciated us not being in their faces, overly exuberant that we won," Koy remembered. "I said, 'Bill, we walked off feeling we were lucky and good. That's a humbling feeling. We walked out knowing we hadn't blown anyone out of the tub.'"

"It seems to me when people talk about the Arkansas game, they always have a story to tell," Street said. "I have had people write me who had heart attacks during the game and the first thing they asked when they came to in the hospital was, 'Who won?' It amazes me that people got that involved in it."

Texas's celebration was short-lived. As Royal and the Longhorn captains were in New York to accept the MacArthur Bowl award as national champions, a medical examination revealed that the pain in Freddie Steinmark's thigh was from a cancerous tumor. His left leg was amputated at the hip.

"When we found out, we were flabbergasted," said Coach Mike Campbell, who would die of complications of lymphoma in 1998. "They said there was just muscle holding the bone together."

Steinmark stayed with the team, serv-

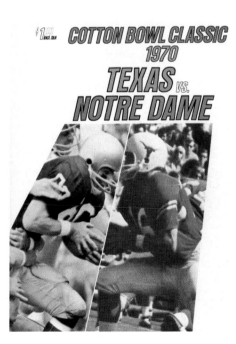

Though Texas had won the UPI national title by beating Arkansas, the Longhorns needed to beat the Irish to earn the top spot in the AP poll.

Irish Coach Ara Parseghian
and Royal talk before
the 1970 Cotton Bowl.

above: Freddie Steinmark
played in pain the last half
of the 1969 season with
what he thought was a
thigh strain.

right: An exam two days
after the victory over
Arkansas revealed
Steinmark had cancer.
He fulfilled a vow
to attend the Cotton Bowl
less than a month after
his leg was amputated
at the hip.

ing as a student coach in 1970. When his hair fell out, he got an earring and joked he was Mr. Clean. Balancing on one leg, he was still able to drive golf balls long and straight. He died on June 6, 1971.

Texas faced Notre Dame in the Cotton Bowl and needed another improbable comeback. Trailing 17–14 with just under seven minutes left, the Longhorns drove 76 yards, twice converting fourth-and-2 situations. On third-and-goal from the 1, Billy Dale scored and Texas won 21–17. Mike Campbell presented Steinmark the game ball in the locker room.

With Eddie Phillips taking over for Street, the Longhorns kept things rolling in 1970, with a 10–0 regular season that included a 42–7 rout of Arkansas in the season finale at Memorial Stadium. Bellard, who wasn't pleased with the way the Razorbacks had handled his offense the year before, made adjustments to the blocking schemes.

"They had a good plan in 1969 and perhaps we, or I, did not adapt as fast as I could have," Bellard said. "The next year, at 'Shootout II,' they came with the same plan and we plumb blew them out of the stadium."

The Longhorns headed to the Cotton Bowl for a rematch with Notre Dame, but this time the Irish were ready. Coach Ara Parseghian had watched film of the previous Cotton Bowl loss, and seeing how easily the Longhorns handled Arkansas in the rematch, devised a different scheme. The Irish mirrored their defense to the Longhorn offense, and forced 10 fumbles and won the game 24–11, ending the Longhorns' win streak at 30.

"I worked with this thing in my mind ever since we played them last year," Parseghian said after the Cotton Bowl. "We learned a great deal about the wishbone last year and we adopted it as one of our offensive sets to learn more about it. After the Arkansas game [in 1970], I knew no standard defense

top: Notre Dame had no answer for the wishbone or for Street's opportunistic passing in the 1970 Cotton Bowl.

middle: Street decides whether to take the first of three options available to him in the wishbone, the give to the fullback. He could also pitch to the trailing halfback or keep the ball himself.

bottom: Ted Koy fights for yardage close to the Notre Dame end zone.

Billy Dale takes a handoff off left tackle for
the game-winning touchdown
against the Irish.

WOOSTER BOOSTERS

Courtesy: BERT'S BAR-B-Q ~ 610 West 19th Street

FOR HEISMANN TROPHY 1970

left: Steve Worster barely practiced before the 1971 Cotton Bowl because of injuries and had four of the Longhorns' 10 fumbles, 5 of which they lost in the streak-ending defeat.

above: Worster finished fourth in the Heisman voting behind quarterbacks Jim Plunkett, Joe Theismann, and Archie Manning, the highest finish since James Saxton was third in 1961.

below: Wishbone creator Emory Bellard's drawing of the game-breaking play against Arkansas in 1969. Bellard diagrammed plays on graph paper to show how easy it was to reach the corner in his triple-option offense.

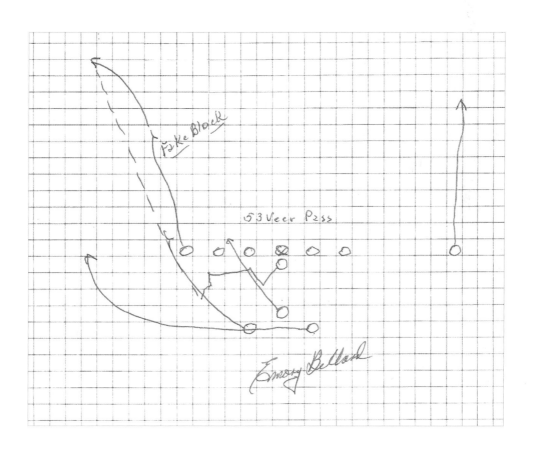

Notre Dame came up with a scheme that neutralized the Longhorns' wishbone, ending the Texas win streak at 30.

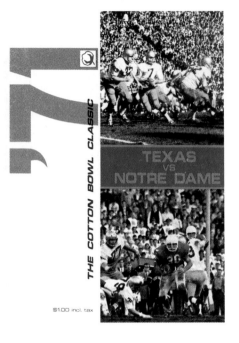

THE COTTON BOWL CLASSIC

TEXAS
vs
NOTRE DAME

$1.00 incl. tax

like you play all year against teams with a split end and a flanker would work against Texas."

While the pain of the defeat by Notre Dame lingered, there was a more pressing loss. The fabled Worster Bunch, an 18-member senior class that had arrived in 1967 and forged a 30-2-1 record over their last three seasons, was gone.

As more schools began using the wishbone, defenses caught up to the intricacies of the triple option. A year later the Longhorns went 8–2, with Arkansas and Oklahoma exacting revenge for their shattering losses of the previous years. In the Cotton Bowl they were dressed down by a Penn State defense that had all the answers for the triple option in a 30–6 rout.

The Longhorns would rise up again with a 10-1 season in 1972, losing only an embarrassing 27–0 decision to Oklahoma, but they would never seriously challenge for a national championship again under Royal, proving their coach more than a little bit prophetic when he said after the Cotton Bowl loss to Notre Dame, "We'll be back with the ordinary people."

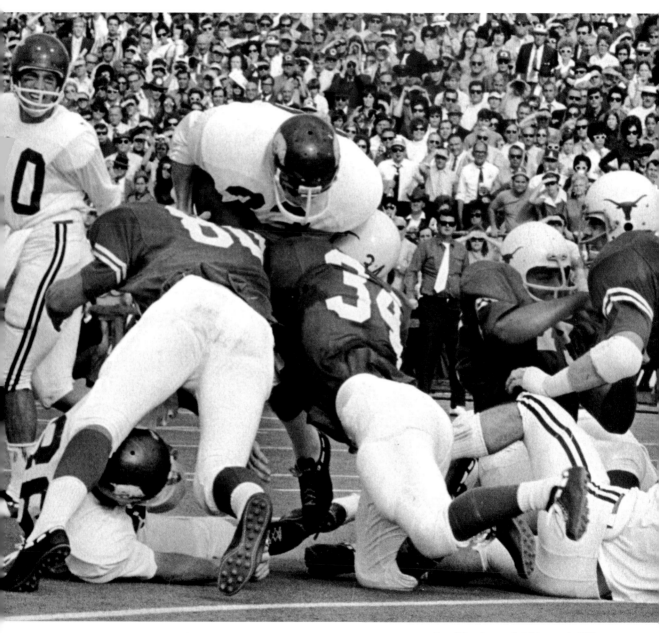

A goal-line stop against Arkansas in 1970 led to a 99-yard scoring drive that keyed a 42–7 rout in Big Shootout II in Austin.

6

OKLAHOMA AIN'T OK

When Randy McEachern finished up his football career at the University of Texas, he chose a future as an investment broker, in which he managed other people's assets.

Not that he didn't have some experience at that.

The annual Texas-Oklahoma game provides one of the most unusual settings in all of sports. The Texas State Fair is swirling around you; the stands are split half-Longhorn, half-Sooner; the crowd is almost on top you and there's an unforgettable trip

through the tunnel to a game you'll remember for the rest of your life. It's unique because of what else it provides—a chance for the heroes to be gods and the nobodies to be heroes. On what's normally the second Saturday of October the floor of the Cotton Bowl is the land of opportunity and on one unlikely afternoon in 1977, McEachern heard its call.

When the Longhorns' top two quarterbacks went down in the first quarter of that game against the Sooners, the slightly built redshirt junior, who had signed to play junior college football before a late scholarship opened at Texas, entered the game in front of a roiled crowd of 72,032. He had one mission—guide the No. 5 ranked Longhorns, who had jumped from a preseason No. 18 into the national title picture in less than a month, to victory against the No. 2 Sooners.

Overlooked in recruiting and coming out of Pasadena Dobie, McEachern was set to enroll at TCU but the Frogs wanted him to go to Navarro Junior College. McEachern had just signed with Navarro when his father ran into a Texas coach who asked where his son was going. The coach invited McEachern to spring practice, and with two late grants-in-aid opening up in the first year of the thirty-scholarship limit, backfield coach Fred Akers offered one to McEachern.

"To this day Ronnie Miksch and I

argue over who was No. 29," McEachern said, "and who was 30."

On moving day his freshman year he was standing with two offensive linemen when senior Doug English drove up and commandeered their services to help him move. He looked over the unimposing McEachern and handed him an inner tube. "Take this to the car," he said. "You other guys, you get the heavy furniture."

McEachern tore knee ligaments early in the 1976 season and spent the Oklahoma game that year spotting for the television announcers. In the spring, Akers, who had taken over as head coach, marked McEachern for defense. "I went in to Coach Akers and said, 'I think I'm as good as any of your other quarterbacks. Give me a chance.'"

Akers relented, but McEachern didn't exactly soar up the depth chart, though he was a solid No. 3 when the season opened.

If he harbored any hopes of playing against Oklahoma that year, it would most likely have been mopping up a Sooners blowout. Texas hadn't beaten Oklahoma since 1970 and the Sooners were only two years removed from their back-to-back national titles.

Akers couldn't expect any quarter from Oklahoma Coach Barry Switzer, whom he played with and coached alongside at Arkansas. Asked about their relationship, Akers said, "We were fairly good friends, but he's not in my will or anything like that."

Responded Switzer, "That's okay. I don't plan on him dying anytime soon."

The playing mortality of Texas quarterbacks, on the other hand, wasn't so encouraging. An early interception on an Earl Campbell halfback pass led to a huge shift in field position that ultimately set up a 47-yard field goal from Uwe von Schamann that gave the Sooners a quick 3–0 lead. Trying to rally the Longhorns, starter Mark McBath was swarmed by Sooner tacklers and broke his ankle. Jon Aune replaced him, but before he could get anything started his knee buckled while he was trying to get past an Oklahoma lineman.

Now it was McEachern's turn. He thought it so unlikely that he'd play that his parents had stayed home. With the Sooners on a probation that barred television appearances outside of Norman and Austin, they listened on the radio as their son entered the biggest game of his life.

The week before he had a dream about playing the Sooners, and told his family. They asked him how it came out. "I don't know," he said. "I woke up before the dream was over."

Now it was no dream.

"Thank goodness our next guy was Randy McEachern," Akers said. "Nobody knew anything about him. But he knew."

The story—one that McEachern did his part to spread—went that McEachern was such an unknown quantity that the Longhorns' star halfback, Earl Campbell, met him halfway on the field and introduced himself. "It makes a great story," McEachern said, "but it's not true."

"Did anybody say anything to me as I went into the huddle?" he recalled. "Yeah. 'Speak up.'"

McEachern had plenty of help. The Longhorn defense contained Sooner Thomas Lott and the Sooners' wishbone, and kicker Russell Erxleben gave Texas a monumental edge in field position, first with a 71-yard punt and later by kicking a 64-yard field goal, only three yards shorter than the NCAA-record boot he made earlier in the season against Rice. McEachern also had Earl Campbell running behind him. Campbell made 114 of his 124 yards after first contact with a Sooner defender.

"Earl did a great job," Akers recalled. "Oklahoma had to play two, maybe three games of defense. It seemed like every time he got the ball, everyone on their team had about two chances to hit him. He wouldn't go down."

McEachern, meanwhile, did what he had to do, completing 4 of 8 passes for 57 yards and staying out of trouble as Texas won 13–6 to move up to No. 2 in the AP poll. Akers, who after he was done coaching formed a leadership consulting firm with his son Danny, the Akers Performance Group, said he'd never seen a team respond after losing its top two quarterbacks like the Longhorns did.

"I talk about that a lot in my talks with businesses, when I speak to teams," Akers said. "Most people give up when their first-team quarterback goes out. Those who didn't certainly did when the second-teamer went out. And there had to be some on our sideline who wondered what the devil we were going to do. Randy dispelled that very quickly."

Even for those who aren't thrust into having to win or lose what's almost always the biggest game on both teams' schedules, the Texas-Oklahoma game is different from any other.

Former linebacker Pat Culpepper was a Longhorn assistant coach, one year removed from his playing days, when he described what the moments before kickoff were like in an article he wrote for the *Daily Texan* in 1968.

"Pregame warm-ups are the hardest thing about the game preparation. You get winded, you feel awkward, and you feel inadequate, but you start feeling mad. It comes with 'Boomer Sooner' and those red jerseys and the cannons going off as OU races out on the field. It's been there before during the week, when you locked yourself away mentally and thought about Dallas. It's been there when you heard people all summer tell you, 'The Big Red is going to get y'all this year'; while you were sweating and working during those hot months; it came when you read about the great OU teams of the past, with their 47–0 scores against Texas while using Texas boys to

win back their 'state pride'; but most of all it rushes to the surface now—and you know that before you leave that field you will play the game of your life."

Culpepper also took a shot at the incongruity of the television introductions before games, when the players are supposed to look into the camera and flash their teeth. "How can you smile before a football game with Oklahoma?" he wrote. "It's like laughing before you land on Iwo Jima."

Halfback Ted Koy is a veterinarian in Georgetown, Texas, and there's a photo hanging on his office wall of him playing against the Sooners. "I'm running the ball and there are bodies everywhere. My shoulder pads are out, my jersey's torn. I love that picture. Against OU every play is a knockdown, drag-out, whoever-gets-up-goes-on-to-win thing. In most games you have butterflies at the start and they go away. That game never settles down. Every play you have to explode."

Darrell Royal, who played for the Sooners in the late 1940s and went 2–2 against Texas, described the game before the teams met in 1969.

"It will be an old-fashioned, country, jaw-to-jaw, knucks-down gut check," he said. "Like when you shot marbles as a kid and then you started playing 'keeps,' and everybody got knucks down, and you hoped the other guy's hand would quiver, and if it didn't, you knew you were all covered up with trouble."

Barry Switzer, who according to assistant Larry Lacewell judged everything his program did on whether it helped them beat Texas, said, "When you beat the University of Texas, I don't care what your won-loss record is, it's the biggest day of your life."

That day, whichever side you end up on, starts with the one thing that every player, whether he wears burnt orange or crimson, will never forget: a trip down the tunnel. It's different for Texas than it is for Oklahoma in that when the Cotton Bowl was split in half for the ticket allocation, they split it at the 50-yard line instead of the middle of the end zones. That means Texas has to parade past Sooner fans every year, a situation Switzer said "makes Texas the visiting team every year."

Koy's father, grandfather, and older brother had all played in the game before he made his debut in 1967, but he still wasn't fully prepared for the experience. "I'll always remember the first OU game I played. It was my sophomore year," he said. "I'd been there before, watching my older brother Ernie. Now I'm coming down the tunnel. I'd heard about it. I'd read about it. I'd seen it. But it was different than anything I expected. You don't hear the crowd, you feel it. You feel like you're standing in front of a giant speaker. I was thinking, 'What in the heck am I getting myself into?'"

"In 1999 there was this old lady who flipped the bird and then threw a Dr.

Pepper bottle at us," former Longhorn guard Beau Baker said. "How many grandmothers resort to violence?"

Once out of the tunnel, the Longhorns have to run past the Ruf/Neks, an Oklahoma spirit group armed with modified 12-gauge shotguns.

"I'd be running out and the Ruf/Neks would be shooting off their popguns, or whatever those things are," former Texas quarterback Peter Gardere said. "They'd stick it right by my ear. Blam. Blam."

Even U.S. presidents aren't immune from the taunts. In 1976, Gerald Ford was flanked by Royal and Switzer when he walked out on the field for the ceremonial pregame coin flip.

"Some redneck from Oklahoma stands up and shouts, 'Who are those two assholes with Switzer?'" recalled Switzer. "It embarrassed the hell out of me. I just kept walking straight ahead. I wanted to crawl in a hole. But if given the opportunity, I'm sure some redneck from Texas would have said that, too."

Royal shakes his head at the story, saying he believes Switzer made it up.

"I think everyone would have known who the president of the United States was," Royal said. "They might have had a question about the other guys."

Maybe somewhere else, but not at the Cotton Bowl in October.

Before concerns about pregame rumbles caused the teams to make substantially staggered entrances, they would both mill in the tunnel before running on the field, exchanging epithets, threats, and the occasional forearm shiver.

"I don't know how many times we'd get into a scrape, with banging, shoving, and elbowing," Akers said. "Luckily we didn't have an out-and-out brawl. Most of the team would have just as soon fight it out in the parking lot, or right there in the tunnel."

Now the only battles in the tunnel are between the spirit groups. During one game in the late 1990s, some Sooners crept past the Longhorn groups guarding the trailer for Bevo, the Texas mascot, during the game and slapped a large padlock on the door. After the game, Bevo had to cool his heels while a bolt cutter was rounded up. After that incident, the Silver Spurs were required to bring bolt cutters.

An enduring feature of the game, along with things like Big Tex, saltwater taffy, and Fletcher's Corny Dogs, is trash-talking.

One year in the early 1960s the talking got so bad that Royal reamed them out after a ragged first half. "Quit mouthing off with them," tackle Staley Faulkner recalled Royal saying. "Don't talk back to them. Play our own game, not theirs."

Oklahoma tackle Ralph Neely took it to the Longhorns in 1962, setting the stage for a verbal counter-barrage the next year.

"We usually don't talk to them,"

tackle Scott Appleton said before the '63 game. "We just concentrate on staying with them. We let them talk and just keep pouring it to them. They've never said much to me. But Neely talked to one of our players and kept saying things like 'you're not worth a darn,' and 'you shouldn't be out on this field,' and 'you're really easy.' But we're out here to beat them, not talk to them."

That, though, was just talk. Quarterback Duke Carlisle remembers that after the Longhorns had pulled comfortably ahead of top-ranked Oklahoma in a game that would put Texas atop the polls, one of his linemen talked back to Neely.

"We were ahead 14–0 and we were running the option play," Carlisle recalled. "I was coming down the line. I heard one of our players say to Neely, 'Who's No. 1 now?' I was thinking, 'Great, we're all gonna get killed by Neely. He's gonna tear the halfback's head off and then he's gonna tear my head off.'"

One of the sorest points in any Longhorn's feelings toward Oklahoma is the number of Texas-bred players who've helped the Sooners beat their home-state university. "Why, that's just like somebody from the United States playing for Nazi Germany," Texas fullback Harold Philipp said in 1963.

Except if you were one of those players, of course. Jerry Tubbs, a center from Breckenridge, Texas, played in the middle of a run from 1948 to 1957 in which the Sooners won 9 of 10. Most of those games were at least close, so when OU humiliated Texas 45–0 in 1956 in a game that sounded the coaching death knell for Ed Price, Tubbs said, "I gotta beat 'em. Everybody from Texas does. I kept thinking I'd sure hate to be playing for Texas and take this kind of humiliating beating."

The exodus peaked in the 1970s and 1980s. The 1974 Sooner team that won the first of back-to-back titles did so with a roster that featured 25 Texans, including All-American halfback Joe Washington.

For the big stage the game provides, its beginning was in fact humble. The teams met in Austin in 1900, with the "Varsity" rolling to an easy 29–2 victory, substituting heavily in the second half. Coach S. H. Thompson had reason to try different combinations—it was widely reported as being a practice game. For Vanderbilt.

"The game yesterday answered admirably for the purpose of showing up the 'Varsity's' weak points and Coach Thompson will spend this afternoon drilling the men where they are weak," read the next day's account in the *Austin-Statesman*.

The story continued, "It is Coach Thompson's wish to send out a team this year that plays the real article. He will not be contented with the mediocre

Oklahoma opened the 1914 game with a kickoff return for a touchdown, the first score Texas had given up all year, but the Longhorns rallied for a 32–7 victory.

OKla game "1914"

playing and neither will the students. The big game Saturday is only two days off, and the men will have to work to beat on that day, Vanderbilt."

The first game lacked gravitas, but the rivalry quickly made up ground.

On one side was Texas, which had once been a sovereign nation, a land of beauty and wealth and, of course, arrogance. On the other was Oklahoma, a state ravaged by the Dust Bowl that caused a mass exodus in the 1930s and gave the state an inferiority complex that was so severe the state slogan became "Oklahoma is OK," as if that was a grand pronouncement of confidence. Even the Sooners' nickname had less than complimentary origins, referring to settlers who jumped the gun moving into the Oklahoma Territory in the

Land Run of 1889. Over the years Oklahoma has recast the nickname into a synonym of progressivism, and in the media guide describes a Sooner as an "energetic individual who travels ahead of the human procession."

John Steinbeck's epic 1939 novel about the hard life in Oklahoma during the Depression, *The Grapes of Wrath,* included this description of an Okie, given to protagonist Tom Joad, courtesy of a random Texan. "Well, Okie used to mean you was from Oklahoma. Now it means you're a dirty son of a bitch. Okie means you're scum."

And that's pretty much the way it stayed for the first 42 games in the series, when Texas won all but 13, losing back-to-back games only three times from 1900 to 1948.

That began to change with the arrival of two men at Oklahoma. President George Cross served as school president from 1943 to 1968. Searching for a positive identity for the university and the school, Cross saw football as the answer, once telling a state legislative committee overseeing educational funding, "I would like to build a university which the football team could be proud of."

The other arrival was Charles Burnham "Bud" Wilkinson, who was named head coach in 1947. Wilkinson had promised his father he'd go into the family mortgage trading business, but his heart was in coaching. An assistant to Jim Tatum, and the backfield coach of a

Oklahoma edged Texas 14–13 on the way to the Sooners' first of seven national championships.

COTTON BOWL NEWS, OCTOBER 14, 1950

TEXAS VS. OKLAHOMA

23

OFFICIAL PROGRAM
50c

Texas fell behind
the Sooners 14–0 in 1969
but rallied behind
the passing of James
Street for a 27–17 victory.

versatile back named Darrell Royal in the late 1940s, Wilkinson was moved up to the top job at age 31 when Tatum took the head coaching job at Maryland.

"His teams dispelled the Dust Bowl *'Grapes of Wrath'* image of the Depression years," Cross said. "They made Oklahoma proud and called national attention to the state's potential."

Just as important, Wilkinson learned to beat Texas. After dropping a 34–14 decision to the Longhorns in his first season, Wilkinson won 9 of the next 10, a streak marred only by a 9–7 loss in 1951. The Longhorns won with one of the greatest defensive efforts in the series and without halfback Gib Dawson, whose father had suffered a heart attack and died while he was visiting with his son as they were preparing to board the bus to the game.

The Longhorns' fortunes changed when they hired Royal in 1957. Royal had barely been introduced as the new coach when Board of Regents Chairman Tom Sealy asked, "Now, Coach, who's the first team we're going to beat?"

Royal knew the right answer: Oklahoma. Instead, he gave the correct one. "I think we open with Georgia," he said with a smile.

Wilkinson gave his former star a rough introduction in 1958, beating him 21–7, but Royal was ready in 1958. Hav-

Dallas has hosted
the annual matchup,
first at Fair Park Stadium
and later at the historic
Cotton Bowl, the site of
many of the Longhorns'
biggest victories.

ing played on the other side of the rivalry, Royal knew immediately what it would take to beat his old school. "The only way anyone's going to beat Oklahoma is to go out there and whip them jaw to jaw," he said. "They get a yellow dog running downhill and they strap him pretty good."

OU was running a new, hybrid offense in 1958, which combined a spread T-formation with a fast break attack that the Sooners had popularized. OU would send the center out over the ball, a receiver to each side, and then hold the rest of the team back before they ran up to the line and the ball was quickly snapped. The Sooners would run a variety of formations out of the fast break, sometimes moving the entire line to one side of the center.

Oklahoma led 14–8 with 12:58 left, but the Longhorns went on a thirteen-play, 74-yard drive that resulted in a 7-yard jump pass for a touchdown from Bobby Lackey to Bobby Bryant. Texas hung on to win 15–12. Overcome by nerves and the emotion of beating his alma mater and mentor, Royal bent over and threw up leaving the field.

"It was a big win for a young coach," Royal recalls. "It did a lot for my being accepted as head coach by alumni and fans of Texas. It had a lot to do with establishing a program. We hadn't done much up till then. We hadn't had time."

Now the tables were turned. Wilkinson would never beat Texas again and re-

tired after the 1964 season, and Royal won seven of eight. Sly as always, Royal said he envied the Sooners' position as undisputed monarch of the Big Eight while his team was locked in a battle every year for the SWC crown, usually with Arkansas up next after the Sooners. "It's the big game of the year for them," he said. "We're lucky. We get to do it all over again next week . . . then the next week."

Times changed again. Under new coach Barry Switzer, recruiting took on a harder, more aggressive flavor, and Royal no longer had the stomach for it. In 1973 the NCAA hit Oklahoma with two years' probation for recruiting violations, banning them from bowl games in 1973 and '74 and television appearances in '74 and '75. The Associated Press voters, deciding that it wasn't their responsibility to enforce the NCAA rules but to declare a champion based on what happened on the field, voted the Sooners national champions in 1974 and '75.

That has never sat well with Texas players and fans, who are on the short end of the national championship race, seven titles to four.

"They won two national championships while on probation," said former Texas lineman Rick Ingraham, who played in the mid 1970s. "That could never happen today. Those kids were walking around with championship rings and they couldn't even be on TV. I said in 2000, when Bob Stoops won it

*A 15–15 tie on a rain-slicked field
in 1984 left No. 1 Texas relieved;
No. 3 Oklahoma felt cheated.*

all, that was their first clean title. They weren't on probation, not fixing to go on probation, or not coming off probation. Bob Stoops did it the right way."

Royal's final season, in 1976, produced the ugliest incident of the rivalry. Late in the week before the game, Royal told the *Austin American-Statesman* that Oklahoma had been spying on his practices and he could provide a witness. Houston alum Tony Herry fingered Lonnie Williams from nearby Rockwall as the spy. Royal offered to donate $10,000 to charity if Williams and Switzer could pass lie detector tests. Both declined. Royal then offered the money to the men directly. Switzer and Williams denied the charges.

"Why those sorry bastards," Royal said in an AP interview he mistakenly thought was off the record. "I don't trust them on anything."

Texas managed to tie the Sooners that year, 6–6, but Royal had enough, submitting his resignation on the afternoon of the regular season finale against Arkansas.

The 1984 game marked another huge turning point. The Longhorns were No. 1, the Sooners No. 3. Texas trailed 15–12 in the fourth quarter when Kevin Nelson broke a 58-yard run down to the Sooners' 3. But three runs up the middle netted nothing, and Nelson slipped on the slippery and worn turf on a fourth-down sweep. When the Longhorns got the ball back, they drove to the 15, where

Sooners safety Keith Stanberry made an interception in the end zone. Officials ruled he was out of bounds, though replays showed he landed in the end zone. The next play, Jeff Ward kicked the game-tying field goal.

"It's like being a boxing champion," Akers said. "You can't take the title away from the champion unless you beat him."

Switzer was certain the Sooners had; they had just gotten jobbed. "All the calls made against us there at the last were by Southwest Conference officials," said a seething Switzer.

Sooners quarterback Danny Bradley questioned the Longhorns' nerve. "If you're the No. 1 team in the country you go for a win, not a tie. We would have gone for it."

One of the most improbable runs in the series was Texas's four straight wins from 1989 to '92. Only one was decided by more than four points and the Longhorns had to rally for victory in all but one of them.

After the last victory, senior linebacker Lance Gunn held up four fingers to the Sooners crowd and crowed, "Take four of these and call me in the morning."

Quarterback Peter Gardere, who entered the '89 game as a redshirt freshman and rallied the Longhorns, earned a place in Texas lore as the only quarterback ever to go 4–0 against the Sooners. A few years later, Gardere was vacationing with a few former teammates in Buenos Aires,

facing page: Texas ended a five-year losing streak to the Sooners when Johnny Walker made a leaping catch of a late touchdown pass from redshirt freshman quarterback Peter Gardere.

TEXAS 28 · FIG RA · OKLAHOMA 28 · DUTSIDE 89° · DOWN 3 · TO GO 2 · 00:00 · YD LNL 42 · QUARTER 4 · 2 TIME OUTS LEFT · BUD LIGHT · TIME OUTS LEFT 0 · 25

Longhorn fans celebrate the 1989 victory over No. 15 Oklahoma, which started a four-year run of Texas upsets over the Sooners, who were ranked No. 4 in 1990 and No. 6 in '91.

Argentina, when a stranger approached them at a McDonald's and asked, "Aren't you Peter Gardere?"

"My friends turned around and said, 'Oh no. Not again. Not here,'" Gardere said. "After that they started calling me, 'Numero diez, muy famoso.'"

In 1994 the stage belonged to two Longhorns, Stonie Clark and James Brown. Brown, a highly recruited but erratic practice player, looked to get his first ever start against the No. 16 Sooners after starter Shea Morenz sprained his knee the week before against Colorado.

"Me and [third-teamer] John Dutton were warming the team up and Shea was on the bicycle, but I knew they'd find a way to get Shea in," Brown recalled. "We said the prayer and coach John Mackovic said, 'James is going to be the starter.' I didn't have time to get nervous."

Brown completed 17 of 22 passes for 148 yards and a touchdown and ran for another score, after which he pumped arms repeatedly and screamed at the crowd—something he didn't even remember doing until he saw the highlights.

Brown's glorious debut wouldn't have mattered if not for a fourth-down stop of Sooners halfback James Allen, who tried to score on a reverse on fourth-and-goal from the 3 with 43 seconds left. Clark lowered his shoulder and spun Allen into the ground a foot short to preserve the victory.

"At the Sun Bowl, I talked with Doug Flutie," Clark said in 1995, referring to the former Boston College quarterback whose Hail Mary to beat Miami in November 1984 made him a college football legend. "He told me all that people knew him for was that long bomb. He said he feels exactly like I did. It's good to know somebody who's made a big living in my shoes."

What had once almost routinely featured a matchup of top 20 teams turned into a game that had no national implications in the late 1990s, with both teams entering the game unranked in 1997 and '98, the first time neither had been ranked since 1968.

above: Stonie Clark (55) earned a spot in Texas-OU history by stopping James Allen inches short of the goal line late in the 1994 victory.

right: James Brown didn't expect to start against the Sooners even during warm-ups in 1994, but he responded with the kind of star turn the game always seems to provide.

The arrival of Mack Brown in 1998 and Stoops a year later brought the game back to national prominence, though the Sooners proved to be the main obstacle standing between Brown and the return of the Longhorns to the national title hunt. From 2000 to 2004, the Longhorns lost five straight. They lost by routs of 49 points in 2000 and 52 points in 2003. They lost on late-game defensive heroics by Sooner safety Roy Williams, who crashed into Chris Simms as he tried to pass out of his own end zone late in 2001, forcing an interception by Teddy Lehman that was returned for the game-breaking touchdown. They lost when their defense couldn't stop Quentin Griffin or hold an 11-point lead in 2002 and they were shut out in 2004, ending a 281-game scoring streak, the nation's longest.

After that win, Oklahoma center Vince Carter of Waco took the Sooners flag and planted it at midfield, as the crowd chanted, "Five in a row."

The Longhorns ended the streak in 2005, running away to a 45–12 victory. After the game the players took turns trying on the Golden Helmet trophy, which none of them had ever touched. Quarterback Vince Young took a victory

lap, slapping five and hugging the Longhorn fans in the Cotton Bowl's front row.

"The end of the third quarter, the beginning of the fourth, we started to have some fun," tackle Justin Blalock said of the Longhorns' huddle. "We were talking to each other, saying 'We can't let up. We've got to kick them when they're down.'"

Ricky Williams wore No. 37 in 1998 to honor Doak Walker, who had died weeks earlier. Williams pointed to the sky and said, "This is for you, Doak," after each of his two touchdowns.

Chris Simms, shaking hands with Oklahoma Coach Bob Stoops, after a one-sided 2002 loss that left him winless in three starts against the Sooners.

115

OKLAHOMA AIN'T OK

The tide had turned again, but bigger and more vital changes were in the offing. After the 2005 game it became apparent the tradition of holding the game at the Cotton Bowl during the State Fair was running out of time. With the Cotton Bowl stadium outdated, and Dallas waffling on making the improvements needed to keep the game, it appeared a foregone conclusion that the series would move to a home-and-home series for the first time since 1929. Then, to the surprise of most observers, in early May 2006 the schools signed a contract extension to keep the game in Dallas until at least 2010.

The tradition lived, the split crowds and the festivities, and the most important thing—a place for the underdog to get back on top, the victim to become the victor.

"That's the thing I tell my kids, other kids," McEachern said. "I'm third string and I'm not getting to play and the next thing you know this happens. You never know. Be prepared."

McEachern's talks may hit a little too close to home. Son Hays is a quarterback, like his father, and was also not highly recruited despite a stellar career at Austin High School. Though he was fed burnt orange like it was breast milk, his parents even taking him to watch the Longhorn band practice on Thursdays before games, he faced an uneasy decision coming out of high school. Air Force offered a full ride but the military commitment did not appeal to him. Sev-

eral schools, including Texas, Auburn, and Texas A&M, invited him to walk on. So did Oklahoma.

Hays chose the Sooners.

"He didn't mention it, but I think he wanted to do his own thing. I think in the back of his mind he was thinking, 'Am I going to get an opportunity just because of my dad?'"

Jenna McEachern, an editor who had worked with Texas Coach Mack Brown on his book *One Heartbeat,* sent Brown a letter explaining it was Hays's decision and that there were no hard feelings. Brown sent one back saying the feeling was mutual.

Randy McEachern, meanwhile, thought of the crazy world of conspiracy theories, and joked about what some Sooners were probably suspecting

"The son of a former UT player and a cheerleader going to Oklahoma?" he said. "You can imagine the OU fans thinking we're planting a spy over there."

By the time the teams met in 2004, Hays had finished his redshirt year and was the Sooners' third-team quarterback, and was a popular interview subject leading up to the game. One reporter asked him if he'd ever seen video of his dad's exploits against Oklahoma. He hadn't, he explained, saying that his mother had been searching for a tape for more than twenty years.

One day a man showed up with a videotape of the game.

"My wife gave it to me for Christmas," McEachern said. "I put it on the VCR and I was like, 'What the heck?' Like I tell everybody, the story's better when there's no tape."

Jenna got the last word. "Remember when Dad said you were a better quarterback than he was?" she told Hays. "Watch this and you'll see it's true."

The McEacherns got to the 2005 game in Dallas. They pulled for Texas but they knew Hays could at any time be called upon to be Sooner hero. His father draws the line at wearing crimson, though Hays has approval to do all things Sooner, with only one caveat. He can never give the upside-down "Hook 'em" sign.

"We are still paying for his education," Randy McEachern said.

Billy Pittman's early touchdown catch helped the Longhorns turn the series momentum with a 45–12 catharsis in 2005.

7

FINDING
DARRELL

When he retired in 1976, Darrell Royal was considered as much a Texas treasure as the Alamo or Old Spindletop. The converted Okie went 167–47–5, captured three national championships, and put Texas on the short list of national powers. He vacationed with LBJ; played golf with Bob Hope; visited Gregory Peck on the set of *To Kill a*

Priest Holmes's touchdown in the Sun Bowl victory over North Carolina was one of the high points in the peak-and-valley tenure of Coach John Mackovic.

Mockingbird; and hung out with Willie Nelson and Larry Gatlin. Whatever he had, he had earned.

At the time, those perks would have appeared to include the chance to name his own successor. His mentor, Bud Wilkinson, did it at Oklahoma, as did the greatest coach Texas had employed before Royal, Dana X. Bible.

Only nobody asked.

"I was not on the selection committee," Royal recalled. "Nobody asked my opinion. I was the athletic director and I was never asked to even be on the selection committee. I never sat and visited with the people in control."

Former governor Allan Shivers, then chairman of the Board of Regents, and university president Lorene Rogers were those people. Texas was entering a new era, and where Royal represented a laidback folksy coach who sometimes had Nelson give concerts in the T-Room for the Longhorn players, they wanted a more polished, sophisticated look.

Defensive coordinator Mike Campbell, a good-natured man whose football acumen was unquestioned, was cut from the same bolt as Royal. They interviewed him six days after the job opened, but by then they had already zeroed in on their top choice, former Longhorn assistant Fred Akers.

Like Royal, Akers built himself up from a background of poverty, growing up in Blytheville, Arkansas, as one of nine children. A quick study, Akers was also a natural athlete who claims to have lost only four football games from the time he was in fourth grade until he graduated from Arkansas in 1960. Trim, personable, and always well dressed, Akers exuded polish and confidence. In two seasons at Wyoming, he had taken the Cowboys from 2–9 his first season to 8–4 and a spot in the Fiesta Bowl, their first bowl appearance in nine seasons.

Ironically, it was Campbell who first brought Akers to Royal's attention. Three years after taking his first job at Edinburg, where at 22 he was youngest high school head coach in the state, Akers was named head coach at Lubbock High, territory that was recruited by Campbell.

"Whenever he was in town we got the projector, some film and plenty of chalk," Akers recalled. "We locked the door and talked football."

When Royal made some staff changes after the 1965 season, he asked his assistants for potential candidates. Campbell mentioned Akers, who was hired as offensive backfield coach. In nine seasons at Texas, Akers developed a reputation as future head coaching material and when the Wyoming job opened in 1974, the Cowboys called Akers.

Akers remembers the Wyoming officials being sensitive about being used as a stepping stone. They asked Akers point blank if that was his intention.

"I told them, 'First of all you haven't offered and I haven't accepted it,'" he

Fred Akers won 73 percent
of his games and didn't
lose in September in his
first nine seasons at Texas.

121

FINDING DARRELL

said. " 'But if I do become head coach I want to make it strong enough you'd want me to stay.' To be honest, there were only two jobs I would have left for—the University of Arkansas and University of Texas. I had no idea both would be open in two years."

When Frank Broyles retired in 1976, Arkansas made some feelers but nothing official developed. Texas, meanwhile, was very interested. Akers traveled to Dallas, where he met with Rogers, Shivers, Athletic Council chairman J. Neils Thompson, and system chancellor Dr. Charles A. LeMaistre. Popular sentiment still favored Campbell, and even Akers at first thought he'd be the choice, if he wanted it.

"I assumed that Darrell would recommend Mike, but I wasn't sure Mike was interested," Akers said. "Mike was one

of the most unpretentious people I'd ever been around. When he talked about it, and maybe he was holding back, he said he didn't want to go through all the hassles. He just wanted to coach."

On the morning of December 15, 1976, eleven days after Royal's last game, a banner headline in the *Austin Citizen* read, "It's Mike." Hours later, the 38-year-old Akers was introduced as head coach.

"I offered Mike to stay on. He told me he thought he was through coaching and would go to work in the athletic department," Akers said. Had Campbell accepted, he would have been defensive co-coordinator with Leon Fuller, whom Akers had brought with him from Wyoming.

"They were so much alike," Akers said of Campbell and Fuller. "If you cut their brains open, a bunch of little defensive players and schemes would run out."

Campbell declined, instead taking a position with the Texas Teacher's Retirement System and then the Texas Longhorn Educational Foundation, where he worked until he died in June 1998 from complications of lymphoma.

Akers inherited a talented team, particularly a sophomore class that included Johnnie Johnson, Johnny "Lam" Jones, Ricky Churchman, and Steve McMichael. Royal realized he was nearing the end of his coaching days in 1975, and made an extra effort to make sure he didn't leave the cupboard bare for his successor.

Akers also switched to a multiple attack that used the I-formation and elements of the veer. He switched Earl Campbell from fullback to halfback and Lam Jones to flanker, where he could join split end Alfred Jackson in stretching defenses.

Texas began the season ranked 18th,

but after edging Oklahoma in Dallas they were up to No. 2. When No. 1 Michigan was upset 16–0 by Minnesota on October 22, the Longhorns were back atop the AP poll, where they hadn't been since December 8, 1970.

First, though, the Longhorns had to get by Arkansas. Third-teamer Randy McEachern, now the starting quarterback, had a week to think of the Razorbacks—and nothing else.

"There wasn't any pressure for the Oklahoma game," McEachern said. "It came next week. Now I was expected to win and we were going to Fayetteville."

The game started as a battle of two of the nation's three best field goal kickers. Russell Erxleben connected from 58 and 52 yards but Steve Little, who along with Texas A&M's Tony Franklin made 1977 the greatest year for placekicking in NCAA history, hit from 33, 67, and 45 yards. The second kick gave Little the satisfaction of tying the NCAA mark Erxleben had set earlier against Rice.

On third down late in the game

Texas's dream for a fourth national title imploded amid six turnovers in a 38–10 loss to No. 5 Notre Dame.

McEachern faked a reverse and threw a screen pass to Campbell, who rumbled down to the 1, setting up the go-ahead and eventual winning touchdown by Johnny "Ham" Jones, so nicknamed to distinguish him from "Lam" Jones.

McEachern remembered the relief of the Longhorns when they got the ball back needing only to run out the clock.

"I was trying to call a play and everybody's talking about what they were going to do tonight," McEachern said. "I said, 'Hey, shut up, let's call the play.' Rick [Ingraham] looked over at me and said, 'Don't get cocky on us now.'"

Texas would persevere through the rest of the season, winning with a defense led by Outland Trophy winner Brad Shearer, linebacker Lance Taylor, end Tim Campbell, and defensive back Johnnie Johnson. McEachern sprained his knee and was replaced against TCU by Sam Ansley, who completed only four passes, but two were touchdowns to Lam Jones, including a 56-yarder. When Ansley had to leave the game for a play to get a new jersey, defensive back Ricky Churchman came in and pitched to Ham Jones for a 66-yard touchdown.

"I really thought that 1977 team was the best description of team as any I've coached," Akers said. "Three things had to happen. First the offense had to put the guys who got hurt out of their minds, had to bear down and get more out of themselves. Even more important is the defense has to step up a notch and

you have to win the kicking game. The kicking game, honest, was like having two or three extra guys on defense."

Earl Campbell, who wasn't even among the Heisman favorites when the season began, became the first Longhorn to win the award. Before Campbell, only two Longhorns had finished as high as third, James Saxton in 1961 and Roosevelt Leaks in 1973. Texas finished the regular season 11–0 with a 57–28 rout of Texas A&M, but the polls had stopped naming national champions until after the bowl games. The Associated Press had made the switch in 1965 but UPI resisted until 1974, changing after Alabama became the second UPI champion in four seasons to lose its bowl game.

In the Cotton Bowl against No. 5 Notre Dame, the Longhorns did everything they avoided during the regular season, turning the ball over and giving up big plays. The Irish took advantage of six turnovers, including three McEachern interceptions, and rolled to a 38–10 victory that vaulted them all the way to No. 1 in both major polls.

"I don't think we were ready to play," Jackson told Kirk Bohls and John Maher in *Long Live the Longhorns*. "We were soaking in our 11–0 season too much. We felt like we were unbeatable."

Akers still rues the change in how the champions were picked.

"Two things I never have understood," Akers said. "Why they changed when they pick the champion and why they don't wait until after the bowls to pick the Heisman winner. They just make it more pressure for players and coaches. The fans might love it, but I don't."

Akers paused. "And," he conceded, "there's some selfishness in there."

For the next three years the Longhorns slipped back in the pack and Akers began to develop a trend that didn't sit well with Longhorn fans. After the Notre Dame loss, Texas beat Maryland in the Sun Bowl but then lost to Washington in the 1979 Sun Bowl and North Carolina in the 1980 Bluebonnet Bowl. It was a combination of less than desirable destinations for fans who expected to spend New Year's Day in the Cotton and losses to teams that weren't considered by Texas fans to be among the national elite. Akers's final bowl record at Texas would be 2–7.

In 1981, behind defensive tackle and Lombardi Award winner Kenneth Sims, the Longhorns beat Oklahoma to ascend to the No. 1 ranking, but then turned the ball over seven times and were embarrassed 42–11 at Arkansas. As usual, Texas had uncertainty at quarterback, with Rick McIvor being replaced by former walk-on Robert Brewer. The highlight of the season was a 14–12 victory over Alabama in Akers's only career Cotton Bowl triumph, which allowed the Longhorns to finish the season ranked No. 2 behind unbeaten Clemson.

Fred Akers said his 1983 team was one of the best in college football. "I'm talking about all of college football," Akers said. "Ever."

They had four all-Americans: guard Doug Dawson, linebacker Jeff Leiding, and defensive backs Mossy Cade and Jerry Gray. Five others would join them on the first-team All-SWC team and only two of their first eight opponents, including Auburn, Oklahoma, Arkansas, and Southern Methodist, scored more than seven points against their defense.

The arrival of highly regarded freshman halfback Edwin Simmons of Hawkins, a potentially game-breaking combination of size and speed, gave them an explosive offensive threat. Simmons arrived with a 67-yard touchdown run up the middle against Oklahoma, but hurt his knee the following week at Arkansas.

Before the game Arkansas coach Lou Holtz, admittedly given to hyperbole, still had ethereal praise for the Longhorns, comparing them with a Nebraska team that was on a wire-to-wire run that kept the Longhorns from rising any higher than No. 2. "Nebraska is a great team, but Texas is awesome," Holtz said. "There's some discrepancy about who's the best team in Texas—the Cowboys or the Longhorns. Asking their offensive linemen to make two yards is like asking a tank to crush a peanut. And in all my years of coaching, this is the best defensive team I've ever seen."

Jitter Fields tries to cover a muffed punt by teammate Craig Curry. Georgia recovered and scored, denying the Longhorns another national title.

Heading into the Cotton Bowl on January 2, the Longhorns were in position to beat Georgia and then wait to see if Miami, on a ten-game winning streak since an opening day loss to Florida, could pull an upset over the 11-point favorite Cornhuskers on their home field in the Orange Bowl that night.

Texas's defense held up its part, allowing Georgia only two penetrations into

No. 2 Texas's loss to Georgia kept the Longhorns from moving up to No. 1 when Miami upset top-ranked Nebraska in the Orange Bowl.

the Longhorn side of the 50, which led to a Bulldogs' field goal. The Longhorn offense, meanwhile, continued to sputter, as it had all season, getting only three Jeff Ward field goals out of seven trips inside the Georgia 33.

With less than five minutes left, Georgia's Chip Andrews lined up to punt on fourth-and-17 at his own 34. Fearful of a fake, Akers kept his regular defense on the field, with Curry staying in instead of normal upback Michael Feldt.

The ball was short and it came to Curry and through his outstretched hands. Deep man Jitter Fields tried to dive on the ball, but it dribbled out and into the grasp of Georgia's Gary Moss at the Texas 23. Two plays later quarterback John Lastinger kept on an option right and ran 17 yards untouched for the game-winning touchdown.

"It was like a nuclear warhead went off," linebacker Jeff Leiding said.

Akers remembered talking to Curry after the game. "It looked like he was crying and couldn't explain it. I told him, 'Look, once we open the doors to the media, you know what they're going to ask. All I can tell you is this: You did play your heart out. That one play did not lose the game. Make sure you stand up. You've enjoyed it when they brag on you. They're going to ask you about one play, one of about 80.' But he didn't want to face it. When the media came in he was gone."

Curry avoided the subject for years to come, and his name came up every time Texas worked its way into the national title hunt. In October 2005, with the Longhorns halfway into their national title run, after almost a year of trying, the *Dallas Morning News'* Brad Townsend finally got Curry to sit down for an interview. "I am hoping and praying that they win the national championship this year," Curry told Townsend. "Please, because I am just dying . . . I don't even go to games at this point. I'm afraid that my presence will be like a taboo. Somebody will see me there and throw rocks or something like that."

Akers is quick to defend Curry. "We could still have won the game," he said. "All we had to do was stop them."

That night, Miami pulled off the upset, not that the Longhorn players were much interested by that time.

Twice Akers had come close to national titles, only to see them evaporate in a sea of mistakes. The next year featured an early No. 1 ranking, but then came a 15–15 tie to Oklahoma and a late-season collapse that sent the Longhorns to the Freedom Bowl against Iowa, a game in which they initially voted not to play.

"That was awful. Nobody wanted to be there," Akers said of the 55–15 loss. "Iowa was a good football team—and they wanted to be there. I think the only reason anybody wanted to go at all was because the bowl was in its first year and it was new."

Texas football was entering a long and irreversible downward spiral. When De-Loss Dodds replaced Bill Ellington as Texas athletic director in the summer of 1981, he drove from his home in Manhattan, Kansas, to Austin, stopping near Dallas to visit Ellington. "You only have two problems," Ellington told him. "The basketball coach and the football coach."

Dodds said he figured out what Ellington meant about coach Abe Lemons, but didn't see the problem early with Akers. He remembered alumni coming to him, angry about the direction of the football program and wanting Akers's head.

"If you don't fire Fred, I'll fire you," he remembered them telling him. He also recalled his response. "You better get me fired, because I'm not going to do it."

Akers's status became such a visible topic that an outspoken Oklahoma linebacker, Brian Bosworth, a native Texan who claimed "burnt orange made me puke" and was acutely aware the Sooners were dominating Akers's teams in 1985 and '86, wrote "Fred" on one shoe and "Akers" on the other as a sarcastic show of support. At the 1985 Bluebonnet Bowl, which Texas lost 24–16 to Air Force, a plane flew over the field carrying a sign that read "Fire Fred." Texas alumni, meanwhile, were sabotaging Longhorn recruiting as a drastic means to force Akers's exit.

"Our alums fed it ourselves," Dodds

said. "We were our own worst enemy."

Dodds eventually saw where the program was headed, and that a change needed to be made.

"I didn't see it as Coach Akers's fault. It was the Southwest Conference. It was a bad time to be coach at Texas," Dodds said. "It was not about something happening, it was about where we were going and can we get it back."

Two days after Akers wrapped up an injury-riddled 1986 season 5-6 with a 16–3 loss at Texas A&M, it was business as usual for the coach. Akers spent Saturday morning taping his weekly coach's show at River City Productions in north Austin, where he got a call from one of his assistants telling him Dodds wanted to talk to him. Akers, who was intending to head to San Antonio to scout a playoff game, said he'd stop at the central Austin offices of the sporting goods store owned by former Longhorn trainer and

Oklahoma linebacker Brian Bosworth's shoes offered mock support for Akers. Texas's 47–12 loss to the Sooners in 1986 started a slide that cost the Texas coach his job.

kicker Rooster Andrews and Dodds could reach him there. By phone, Akers was fired.

Asked later at a press conference if he felt he was given a fair shake, Akers said no. Pressed to elaborate, he said, "That's a stupid question," and walked off.

Almost two decades have passed since his dismissal, but Akers still picks his words deliberately when discussing it, and you can sense the pain hasn't totally gone away.

He is asked about the effects of the firing and he doesn't blink. "It probably cost us a national championship," he said. "It took a good while to get over that, I'd say."

In Lubbock, David McWilliams was surprised by the news.

"I didn't think they'd fire Coach Akers. He had three years left on his contract," he said.

McWilliams, who had served as Akers's defensive coordinator until 1985, when he took the head coaching job at Texas Tech, wasn't prepared for what happened. "At Tech I signed a five-year deal that they could reassign me at the end of any year and terminate the deal at the end of five. It was not a very smart contract on my part. But my thinking was, I go there and stay five years, do a good job, and I wouldn't leave to go anyplace outside of Texas. I expected to be at Tech for a while. We bought a house."

The Saturday after Texas's loss to A&M, McWilliams was driving around

*Texas offense frequently settled for field goals
from All-American kicker Jeff Ward,
a criticism that earned Akers
the nickname "Field Goal Fred."*

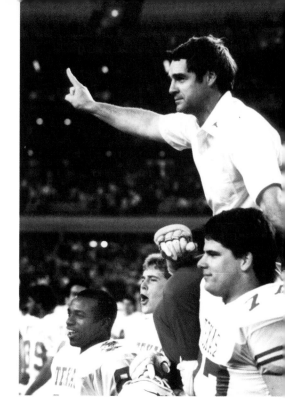

Lubbock, doing errands with his son Corby. They were out to buy Corby a pair of shoes, when a voice on the radio said that the Texas Athletic Council was meeting to consider Akers's future.

"Corby asked me what I would do if they would fire Akers," McWilliams recalled. "I told him that it wasn't going to happen, so there was no reason to think about it. We went in and bought the shoes. We came out and the guy on the radio is saying that Fred's just been fired. We got home and [his wife] Cindy said, 'DeLoss Dodds just called.'"

Dodds had quickly narrowed the search to two candidates. He flew on alumnus Mike Myers's private jet to Phoenix, where he met John Cooper and his family at the Arizona State coach's house. Cooper was interested, but he had just won the Rose Bowl and gotten a nice raise from the Sun Devils, and Dodds said he quickly realized Texas couldn't offer him enough money to make negotiations worthwhile.

Dodds then flew to Lubbock and met with McWilliams. They set up another meeting, with university president William Cunningham and the Athletic Council in Dallas, in an office building near Love Field. The meeting was short. McWilliams was headed back to Texas.

"I remember David telling me, 'If you hire me, I'm not going to wear wingtips. I'm wearing boots,'" Dodds said. McWilliams, of course, could wear

pumps if he did what Dodds and most everybody else expected.

"The university was very fragmented," Dodds said. "Football had not been a fun thing for a long time. David was a healer. He got the lettermen back, the high school coaches back. He gave us a sense of family. David is Texas. David is family. Everybody loved David."

Quarterback Bret Stafford, who played under three different offensive coordinators in his first three seasons of eligibility, said the change in coaching styles was significant.

"Fred is a very classy individual," Stafford said. "I don't know if Fred and I had very good communication. I think we both respected each other. It was his way, no other way. That was the way I was raised, so that was fine with me. There were several times, early in my career when I came off and he'd say, 'I'm going to move you to defensive back next week.' I didn't take that well. Looking back, I think that was Fred's way of making me tougher.

"He was pretty black and white. I liked that. You knew where he was coming from. He didn't get close to you. David felt like one of the guys. It almost felt like he was there with you in the trenches."

One of McWilliams's first goals was to get Royal involved again. For reasons that are unclear even to the involved parties, Royal and Akers drifted apart during Akers's tenure, with Royal feeling Akers didn't want him around and Akers being told he didn't have Royal's support.

"Coach Royal didn't want to come to practice, didn't want people to think he was looking over my shoulder," McWilliams said. "I told him I wanted him to come out and that it would be seen as support."

McWilliams's first season at Texas was a microcosm of his five-year tenure, with staggering losses mixed in with stunning victories. "I remember being worn out from the ups and downs," McWilliams recalled. "One week we'd play well, the next week we would not."

The Longhorns got blown out 31–3 at Auburn in the opener and had seven interceptions in a 44–9 loss to Oklahoma. Then they shocked Arkansas in Little Rock when Stafford hit Tony Jones on an 18-yard post on the game's final play.

The Longhorns then beat Texas Tech and headed to the Astrodome 3–0 in conference play and with a chance to keep alive a Cotton Bowl run against a Houston team that was winless in conference and still trying to figure out a new offense called the run-and-shoot. Texas was leading 34–20 midway through the third quarter, and though Stafford had thrown three interceptions and been knocked out with injuries, backup Shannon Kelley appeared to have the game in control.

Then all hell broke loose. By the time it was over, all four of the Longhorns' interceptions had been returned for touchdowns, three by Johnny Jackson, and four more fumbles led to a 60–40 Cougars victory.

"I didn't only hurt my bad elbow but I hurt the other one," Stafford said. "I told coach someone who wasn't hurting like this could do a better job. It felt like it was splitting right open. I didn't take any Novocain. I wish I would have gotten a shot."

Though the Longhorns still would have to beat A&M in College Station—a game they ended up losing, 20–13—to go to the Cotton Bowl, the Houston defeat still haunts Stafford.

"I sit here twenty years later, and if we had just won that game, we'd have been in the Cotton Bowl. That would have been my only Cotton Bowl."

A 32–27 victory over Pittsburgh in the Bluebonnet Bowl, in which the Longhorns came out throwing deep to split end Tony Jones, gave them momentum heading into 1988. That quickly disappeared when senior Eric Metcalf, a preseason Heisman Trophy candidate, was suspended for the opening game after it was discovered he had accepted tuition money for summer school but hadn't enrolled. Brigham Young routed the Longhorns 47–6, setting the tone for a 4–7 season. Texas lost its fourth straight season opener, this time a 27–6 defeat to Colorado, and 1989 ended in disappointment at 5–6.

In the spring of 1990, twin brothers

Keith and Kerry Cash came to see McWilliams, upset over the constant losing.

"They said, 'We're tired of getting beat,' so I asked them, 'What are your ideas?'" McWilliams recalled.

They suggested early morning workouts, not in the Longhorns' state-of-the-art facility but rather in their dank, dingy old weight room under the grandstands at Memorial Stadium. McWilliams upped the intensity of workouts, having offensive players tackle their defensive counterparts in drills to increase aggressiveness. They stopped interrupting drills to coach players, so as not to disrupt the tempo, and they started every practice with four full speed plays of "inside drill," with the first team offense trying to run between the tackles of the first team defense to set the tone for the day.

Texas went to Penn State and upset the Nittany Lions 17–13, after which sophomore safety Lance Gunn planted the seeds for the season's unofficial motto, screaming, "We shocked the world!"

Colorado, which would win a share of the national title in 1990, rallied to beat Texas 29–24, but Peter Gardere found Keith Cash on a slant pattern and Michael Pollak's point after gave the Longhorns a 14–13 win over Oklahoma. A cathartic, season-making 45–24 victory over No. 3 Houston, which had beaten the Longhorns by 51 and 38

Eric Metcalf was a versatile player who never could seem to find his best role in the Longhorn offense.

Peter Gardere found himself running for his life against Miami in a 46–3 humiliation that ended McWilliams's best season.

Mobil Cotton Bowl

FIFTY FIFTH ANNUAL

DALLAS, TEXAS

JANUARY 1, 1991

Texas vs Miami

far left: Texas's "Shock the Nation" season in 1990 resulted in a matchup with an angry Miami.

left: Oklahoma Coach Garry Gibbs's inability to beat an underdog Texas riled Sooner supporters, but his firing in 1994 sent the program into a tailspin.

points the last two seasons, followed and the Longhorns earned their first Cotton Bowl trip since 1984 by beating Baylor, then they held off a two-point conversion attempt to edge Texas A&M.

McWilliams expected quarterback Bucky Richardson to run the option to the short side of the field, a play Texas had been unable to stop. A&M, though, ran wide, to the right, and linebacker Brian Jones was coming on a blitz called "Red Dog." He forced a quick pitch by Richardson to Darren Lewis. Cornerback Mark Berry, caught in no-man's-land, gambled and came up to make the tackle short of the end zone.

"If Lewis raised up and threw the ball, it would have been an easy touchdown," McWilliams said. "Berry came over and he said he'd read the offensive linemen, knew what the play would be. He made a calculated risk. I told him, 'That's fine. You've got a four-year scholarship. I'm on a year-to-year contract.'"

A matchup in the Cotton Bowl awaited, but an angry Miami, which had uncharacteristically lost two games, was more than a match for an emotionally fat Texas team, blowing them out in what was then the most one-sided game in the 55-year history of the Cotton Bowl despite a record 202 yards in penalties.

In the offseason, as they repeated their 5:30 A.M. workouts, Longhorn players wore T-shirts that read "Never Again." The message was directed at the

lingering sting from the Cotton Bowl, but it just as easily could have referred to the one-hit wonder that was 1990. Texas started with losses at Mississippi State and Auburn, but beat Oklahoma when safety Bubba Jacques took advantage of an offseason rule change that allowed all fumbles to be advanced and took a ball stripped from fullback Mike McKinley 30 yards for what proved to be the difference in a 10–7 win.

The victory was McWilliams's third straight over the Sooners, who had come in ranked 15th, 4th, and 6th. "I always looked forward to that game," McWilliams recalled. "I was always more loose that week. I wouldn't get uptight, I'd cut down on practice. We'd take 'em out of shorts and shoulder pads on Tuesday. It's one of the things I can't explain. I wish I'd had that same feeling, been that way, before every game."

Every game wasn't Oklahoma, and when the Longhorns finished 5–6 and tied for fifth in the SWC, even that goodwill wasn't enough to save McWilliams.

"I felt we'd finally put it together, that it would help us in recruiting," McWilliams recalled. "Ninety-one was really a blow to me because I thought we'd turned the corner. I felt like I couldn't get it going again. I felt like it was time to step down. I got tired. I wasn't burned out. I just felt Texas deserved more than a one-year winning streak."

So did Texas officials, who asked McWilliams to step aside. In retrospect, McWilliams said, he wasn't ready for the job, nor for the demands of overseeing an entire program or, particularly, the media scrutiny a head coach faced.

"I found as a head coach at Tech I had to be careful, because whatever I said was done," McWilliams said. "As an assistant you can say things and they're only suggestions. As a head coach, you say something and people do it. That's when I saw I wasn't ready for it. It wasn't the Xs and Os, it was all the other stuff.

"Another couple years as a head coach would have helped me, no question. If I could have made a timeline, I would have had a couple more years as head coach before I came to Texas."

Three coaches showed up on Texas's short list: Bobby Ross of Georgia Tech, Terry Donahue of UCLA, and John Mackovic of Illinois. Dodds said Ross dropped off the list after a highly televised confrontation with officials in a game with North Carolina. "Terry Donahue was a wonderful man and there was no better football coach," Dodds said. "He just seemed burnt out. I was sitting there talking to him, about football and academics, knowing Texas is another UCLA."

That left Mackovic. A former Dallas Cowboys assistant and head coach of the Kansas City Chiefs, Mackovic built a name as a brilliant offensive coach. He also had a reputation for having prob-lems getting along with players. Dodds said Texas checked out those reports, starting with Chiefs owner Lamar Hunt. "We got a good recommendation," Dodds said. "You never know who to listen to, so you go with your gut."

A wine connoisseur, Mackovic served many of his relationships like he did chardonnay: chilled. He purposely kept Royal and his legacy at arm's length. He did nothing to foster good relations with Texas high school coaches—the life-blood of recruiting—and turned down many of the public appearances Long-horn coaches had always done. He de-creed that only former players who had earned their degrees could come back to use the training facilities. A rumor spread that he was even considering changing the Longhorn logo on the hel-met.

Ted Koy, a halfback on the 1969 na-tional championship team, had enjoyed watching practices under McWilliams, and had hoped to enjoy the same privi-lege under the new coach. Recalled Koy, "His statement was 'Y'all had your turn. We're building our own tradition. If you want to come out, you can sit in the stands with everyone else.'"

Mackovic's first two teams tied for second in a weak SWC, finishing 6–5 and 5–5–1, making 1994 a make-or-break year. It turned out to be both, with one of the wackiest and most amazing single-season rides in history.

It started with preseason suspensions

*Priest Holmes's touchdown capped
the Longhorns' stunning upset of Nebraska in
the 1996 Big 12 championship game,
the high point of John Mackovic's
six seasons at Texas.*

of receivers Mike Adams and Lovell Pinkney. On October 1, Mackovic's fifty-first birthday, he took a helmet under the chin from Tony Brackens as the Longhorn end chased a Colorado ball-carrier out of bounds. Mackovic got a concussion and six stitches, but swore he was fine. "My health is not an issue," he said afterward. "We'll get over it by midnight."

Led by James Brown, Texas beat Oklahoma, but that was the last good news the Longhorns would have for a month. Seven black players were suspended for breaking curfew before the Rice game, splitting the squad along racial lines because several white players who were also out that night were not disciplined. The Longhorns argued on the bus ride to Rice and then on a rainy Sunday, before a captive national television audience made possible by the Major League Baseball strike, they lost to Rice for the first time in 29 games. After an embarrassing loss to Texas Tech, *Austin American-Statesman* columnist Kirk Bohls called for Mackovic's job.

His back against the wall, Mackovic employed the services of media consultant Lisa LeMaster, who advised him to "define yourself or you will be defined." Before a rare early November game with A&M, he told the media he had been suffering from postconcussion syndrome and at the traditional Hex Rally, he wore blue jeans and a pressed white shirt and painted his face. He laughed when safety

Well-groomed, businesslike, and with a love of fine wine, Mackovic didn't fit the image of a Texas football coach.

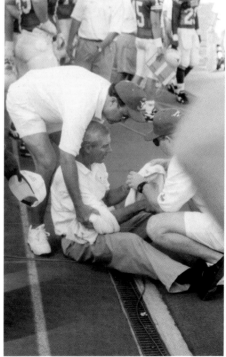

John Mackovic took a helmet under the chin in a sideline collision against Colorado, giving him a concussion and starting one of the oddest one-month runs in Texas history.

Ricky Williams scores the first of his 75 career touchdowns, which was an NCAA record until it was broken in 1999 by Travis Prentice of Miami (Ohio).

Tre Thomas did a spot-on Mackovic impersonation at the team Christmas party.

"At first I thought there was no way in hell this was happening," linebacker Robert Reed said after the season. "When Coach Mackovic first got here, everyone was so uptight. We didn't know what to expect from him; he didn't know what to expect from us. We've taken some long, big strides. At one point we were headed for a big ol' divorce. Now it's a big happy marriage."

On a more tangible level, Mackovic gave the starting job to James Brown, who became only the second black quarterback in school to be a regular starter, and he responded by leading the Longhorns to the Sun Bowl, where they earned a 35–31 come-from-behind victory over Mack Brown's North Carolina team.

The next season the Longhorns won the final SWC title with a 16–6 victory at Texas A&M, in which Brown played on a badly sprained ankle. In the locker room after the game, as the Longhorns celebrated a berth in the Sugar Bowl, a triumphant Mackovic shouted, "Free at last, free at last, thank God almighty, free at last."

Texas lost to Virginia Tech, less than forty-eight hours after discovering reserve defensive back Ron McKelvey was really a 28-year-old former Sacramento State player named Ron Weaver, but carried the momentum to 1996, when they were ranked No. 8 in the preseason,

their highest since 1984. The Longhorns started 3–4, but rallied to win the Big 12 South and, in one of the greatest upsets in conference championship history, beat No. 3 Nebraska 37–27.

Mackovic hadn't yet returned the Longhorns to the promised land, but he was holding his own against Oklahoma (2–2–1) and had turned around the A&M series and taken Texas to two Bowl Alliance games.

Then came UCLA in Austin on September 13, 1997. Texas went in ranked No. 11 and looked at it as a landmark game.

"Even though we beat Nebraska and won the Big 12, we still weren't getting national respect," linebacker Anthony Hicks said. "That was the game that was going to put us on the map. When we lost two heartbreakers to Notre Dame in '95 and '96, two opportunities to put us on the national scene, we let that slip away. This was another chance. That game was going to set the tone for the season. And it did."

UCLA crushed Texas 66–3, a loss only surpassed by a 68–0 rout by Chicago in 1904.

"It was the worst beatdown I've ever been a part of," Hicks said. "It got to the point people were looking at the clock saying, 'Can we get this thing over with?' It was embarrassing, humiliating."

Mackovic, in a remark that would seal his fate in the eyes of many Longhorn supporters, said stiffly, "Last year

Four years after his post–Sun Bowl handshake,
Mack Brown would inherit Mackovic's spot at Texas.

we won this [Big 12] championship and everybody lived with that. They'll have to live with this, too."

Recalled Hicks, "You've got to understand what he was trying to say, that you have to take the good with the bad. But you've got to be truthful and say, 'No, we just got our asses beat.'"

Texas lost five of the next seven. Fans at Oklahoma State, Missouri, and Baylor all tried to tear down the goalposts. On a shelf near his desk, next to coaching biographies and books on management styles, Mackovic kept a small prescription bottle with a cartoon label that read, "More Time." His had run out. Less than twenty-four hours after losing to Texas A&M, 27–16, Mackovic was reassigned.

"What I want is a top ten program and a national championship once in a while," Dodds said at the press conference announcing the change. "I think we can be in the top ten, top fifteen year in and year out and in the top five and win a national championship every once in a while."

Dodds added, "We will go after the best football coach in the country, wherever he is. Somebody who wants to be at Texas."

The pressure was on Dodds. He had fired basketball coach Abe Lemons, then one of the most popular figures in Texas history. His choice to succeed him, Bob Weltlich, had a dry sense of humor that escaped fans and was a martinet in the mold of his mentor Bob Knight, but without the success. Tom Penders proved to be a good hire as his successor, but his reign disintegrated in early 1999 in the midst of a player revolt and charges of improperly released grades. Cliff Gustafson, then the winningest coach in college baseball history, had been forced out in the summer of 1996 after allegations of improper allocation of summer camp revenues.

Dodds was running out of chances. He had to get this hire right.

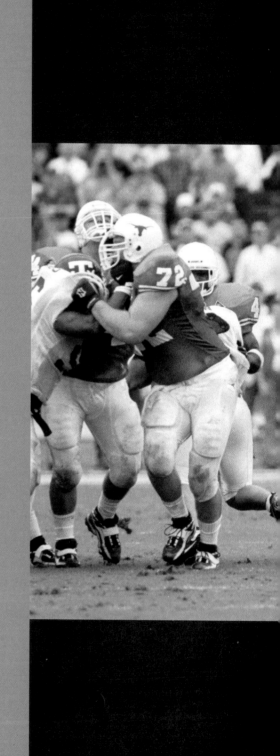

8

LOATHE THY NEIGHBOR

The roots of one of the greatest in-state rivalries in college football run deep and far. It started, like many disagreements, over money. Texas A&M was opened as a land-grant institution in 1876, eighteen years after the state approved the formation of the University of Texas but seven years before the Austin school was established. Yet A&M has always been treated by the state more as a stepchild than as a favorite elder son.

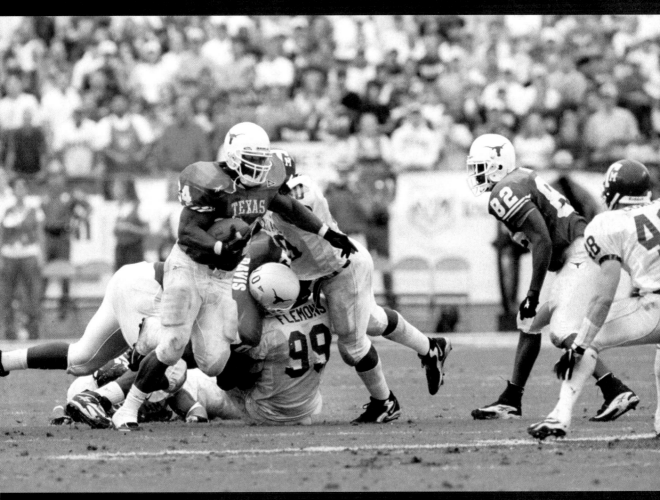

Ricky Williams broke Tony Dorsett's NCAA career rushing record against the Aggies in 1998, though Texas needed a late Kris Stockton field goal for a come-from-behind victory.

While the University of Texas thrived in the 1880s, state officials wondered whether it was feasible even to keep A&M going. When oil was discovered in 1923 at Santa Rita, on land that belonged to the University of Texas, A&M reluctantly agreed to become part of the state system and share in the oil revenue pool, called the Permanent University Fund. By 1931, when the legislature voted to give Texas a two-thirds share and the rest to A&M, the fund was growing by more than $2,000 a day.

A tone was set. While the Longhorns felt entitled, the Aggies yearned for vindication.

It's a rivalry that at times has been very ugly, as when it forced a cancellation of the game from 1912 to 1914. Yet at other times it's become a heartfelt arm-in-arm union, as in the days after the deaths of twelve current and former A&M students in the collapse of the bonfire in November 1999.

Unlike the Oklahoma rivalry, where the one constant is untempered animosity, the Texas–Texas A&M rivalry is often in the eye of the beholder. There are differences, and not just in the way each school prefers to accessorize its pressed khakis—with cavalry sabers and polished boots or polo shirts and Top-Siders.

"Oklahoma in one aspect is a bigger rivalry," Ted Koy said. "It's two bordering state institutions, playing in front of a crowd that's half Texas and half Okla-

homa, at the state fair, with all that hubbub. It's more of a national rivalry. Texas A&M is more your backyard neighbors."

"In rivalry games, sometimes a team has a run, and if you're not careful, then it's natural to say it probably means more to A&M than Texas," Greg Davis, who's been offensive coordinator at both schools, said when the Longhorn run reached six straight in the early 2000s. "The truth is it doesn't, except if you're A&M you want that run to stop."

If, like Duke Carlisle, you attended when the Longhorns were 4–0 against the Aggies and beat them by an average of 11 points, you remember it one way. "When I went to school A&M wasn't a very good team," said the quarterback of the 1963 national champions, whose team needed a fair bit of luck to get by the Aggies during the title year. "Even though it was a huge rivalry and we treated it that way and there was a big buildup, Arkansas and Oklahoma were better teams. Those rivalries were probably bigger than A&M. When it's not a big tough game, it's not as big for the fans."

If, say, you are Bret Stafford and went to Texas in the mid-to-late 1980s and never knew what it was like to beat A&M, you think this: "I don't know if I ever will be able to forget that."

Living in Texas, it's more likely you won't get that chance, either.

"Oklahoma fans, you don't necessarily know them, but they're the enemy," Koy said. "Oklahoma, if you get beaten by them or you beat them, you really don't have to deal with it until the next year. With A&M, you deal with it today, tomorrow, and the next day."

Koy, son, brother, and grandson of Longhorn players, grew up in Bellville, which is only sixty miles from the A&M campus.

"I remember at Bellville Elementary, the principal barred A&M and Texas jerseys because we'd have fights," Koy recalled. "And this was second grade. Instead of a football game, we'd have shirt-pulling and scuffling. That went on for the rest of the year."

Koy also had the unusual experience of attending both schools. After finishing at Texas in the spring of 1970, he enrolled at Texas A&M because it boasted the state's best veterinary school.

"They gave me a hard time and I gave it right back," Koy said. "Every year around the game I'd get calls or I'd call them. Most of the heads of the departments were old Aggies, gone through B.S., M.S., D.V.M., and Ph.D. at Texas A&M. At A&M, if the Aggies beat Texas, then the following Monday is a school holiday. On Monday after A&M won [in 1975], I showed up and Dr. Joyce said, 'Us Aggies have time off— you Tea-sips have to go to school.'"

When it came to grief, early in the series it was the Longhorns who were giving and the Aggies who were taking. The

first meeting between the teams came in 1894, the first game of Texas's second season and the Aggies' first. The score was recorded as 38–0 in the Texas and A&M records; 48–0 in the *Austin Statesman* account. Either way it wasn't much of a game.

"The Varsity boys played like champions and went through the visitors like a temperance resolution at a prohibition convention," read the *Statesman*'s report.

Of the 75 members of the Corps of Cadets who made the trip to cheer their schoolmates on, the *Statesman* said, "At the close of the game they were worse off than ever and looked as if they had swallowed a Sunday school class and the teacher was still sticking in their throats. Some of them even looked worse than that, and were on the verge of beaching themselves when honest hearts and willing hands interfered and prevented the calamity."

The rivalry took its first serious turn when Charley Moran became the Aggies' head coach in 1909. Moran's Machiavellian approach left few stones, or ringers, unturned. Frequently he took advantage of the rules of the day that allowed anyone to play as long as they'd gone to class for a day. Moran supplemented his roster with players from the Haskell Indian Institute in West Texas. A&M, which had won only one of the first seventeen games in the series, shut out the Longhorns in Moran's first two seasons and won 14-8 in his third. The games were also marked by brawls between the fans.

By 1911, the Longhorns were concerned about the nature of the rivalry. Texas students fueled the fire by writing a song about the Aggie coach:

To hell, to hell with Charley Moran,
And all his dirty crew.
If you don't like the words of this song,
To hell, to hell with you.

A large group of Texas fans headed to the game. Those who couldn't get tickets went to a downtown Austin theater and paid 25 cents to hear updates delivered by telegraph.

The game turned on one play. A&M halfback A. R. Bateman was tackled by Frost Woodhull and fumbled. Aggie center George Barnes went to pick up the ball. Texas fans say he bobbled it. A&M supporters contended he was illegally pushed aside by Arnold Kirkpatrick. What wasn't disputed was that Kirkpatrick picked up the ball and ran about 15 yards for the game-winning score.

Texas fans, fearing a celebration rally in Houston would lead to a riot, came back to Austin to celebrate. Since 1909, when Moran arrived, the rivalry was marked by charges of ineligible players and dirty play, but no reason was given when athletic department chairman W. T. Matcher announced the series was suspended. Instead, a brief statement was issued to A&M officials that read, "I beg to inform you that the Athletic Council of the University of Texas has decided not to enter in athletic relations with the Agricultural and Mechanical College of Texas for the year 1912."

The Aggies who branded Bevo with the 13–0 score of the 1915 game pose with their transportation and the tools of their deed.

Two events caused the rivalry to be resumed in 1915. One was the formation of the Southwest Conference, which regulated eligibility and also introduced a change to the series, making the games home-and-home. Before that, every game had been played either in Austin or at a neutral site. The other was the dismissal of Moran, not an easy move because of his popularity among Aggies. Texas officials denied that was a condition for the resumption of the series, though boosters openly vowed they'd never play A&M as long as he was still the Aggie coach.

A&M, though, quickly got a measure of revenge and it involved the Longhorn mascot Bevo. In 1911, Texas manager Stephen Pinckney collected $1 each from 124 students and bought a brown and white steer, which proved too rambunctious to be a proper mascot. Students decided to brand him with the score of the 1916 victory over A&M during a Texas Exes meeting on March 2. A group of Aggies got wind of the plan and sneaked into his pen and branded him with 13–0, the score of the Aggies' victory in 1915.

What happened next is of some dispute. The popular story is that the Longhorns doctored the brand to read "BEVO," which became the steer's new name. The official Texas account, however, is that Ben Dyer, editor of the school's alumni magazine, named the steer when he was given to the school,

saying "His name is Bevo. Long may he reign!"

Why "Bevo"? The two theories explaining Dyer's inspiration are (1) Bevo was the name of a popular nonalcoholic beer and (2) a cartoon of the time had popularized nicknames with an "o" at the end. Dyer had taken a slang word of the era for cow, *beeve,* and added the extra vowel.

Either way, the rivalry had a new element: the mascot as fair game. Bevo was taken again in 1963 and 1971, but the Aggies' dog Reveille was untouchable. That was until 1993, when a group of Longhorn students who called themselves "The Rustlers" took Reveille VI from the Dallas backyard of her handler a few days before the Aggies played Notre Dame in the Cotton Bowl. The dognappers issued their demands to the *Austin American-Statesman,* saying all they wanted was for the Aggies to admit Texas was superior and for A&M quarterback Corey Pullig to flash the "Hook 'em Horns" sign before the game.

A&M, predictably, refused to give in,

A branded Bevo eventually became dinner for both teams, who met for a barbecue in January 1920.

though the Aggies did hold a press conference to announce the disappearance. That, apparently, was enough for the Rustlers, who tied the puppy to a "No Trespassing" sign at Volente Beach near Austin and telephoned a local radio station with her whereabouts. Some Aggies pressed for the state attorney general's office to pursue charges, and Texas president Robert Berdahl issued a statement that read in part, "This entire incident is a stupid, puerile act. If it was perpetrated by UT students, as alleged, it has achieved nothing except to embarrass UT."

Many Aggies, however, say Reveille's record is still clean because Reveille VI hadn't yet officially replaced Reveille V, who was retiring after the Cotton Bowl.

The Reveille caper came a year after one of the more daring pranks in the rivalry. No doubt inspired by the A&M school song, which includes the line "Saw Varsity's horns off," vandals broke into Memorial Stadium sometime late on Wednesday, November 18, 1992, and using razors and pliers cut both horns off the Longhorn logo celebrating the centennial of Texas football that was painted at midfield. One horn was found in a flower bed outside the stadium. The other was never found, though rumors were that it was to be placed on top of the Aggies' bonfire.

One of the more creative exchanges happened in August 1996, when 28-year-old A&M alum Michael Kelley of Pflugerville used the guise of the Texas Public Information Act to file a request for the Longhorn playbook.

Berdahl, taking this prank much less seriously, fired back by recalling the inscription of the flag carried by Texicans in the Battle of Gonzales. "That flag had a picture of a cannon on it and the words, 'Come and take it.' If we have to update that flag with a playbook I'm prepared to," Berdahl said.

Kelley didn't pursue his request, but the editors of the *Daily Texan,* the student newspaper in Austin, joined the fray, filing their own open records request. A&M associate vice president of finance Richard Lloyd sent a letter back to the paper promising that "a graphic illustration of the requested information will be available for your inspection on Nov. 29, 1996, at approximately 10 a.m." That was kickoff.

Lloyd also eschewed any historical references in his reply, instead using a poem that pleaded for leniency based on the Aggies' 0–2 start that season.

We are the Aggies, the Aggies so blue
We need our playbook more than t.u.

It didn't help. Texas won 51–15.

When the series had resumed in 1915, the Aggies—who had had received a telegram from Moran saying that if "you still love me and think anything of me, you'll beat Texas"—had won 13–0. It wasn't the same series, though. Fans,

happy the series was back, sang "Auld Lang Syne" before the kickoff and carried both teams from the field after the game. The Corps of Cadets marched in a T formation as a show of respect of Texas.

In 1939 Homer Norton had built a power around All-American fullback John Kimbrough and the Aggies rolled over Texas 20–0 on the way to A&M's only national championship. The following year A&M came to Texas riding a 20-game winning streak and as a four-touchdown favorite, a near lock to earn

their first-ever victory in Memorial Stadium. On the fourth play of the game, Noble Doss made an over-the-shoulder catch down to the 1; quarterback Pete Layden scored on the next play and the Texas defense held, giving the Longhorns a 6–0 victory that denied the Aggies a second national title.

In 1941 the Longhorns were still ruing a late-season tie to Baylor and a loss to TCU that would ultimately keep them from their first-ever bowl appearance when they played the unbeaten No. 2 Aggies in College Station. The Long-

above: Bad blood between the schools caused the rivalry to be interrupted from 1912 to '14, but when it came back to Austin in 1916 the Clark Field stands were full.

below left: A&M came into the game as defending national champions and with a 19-game winning streak but left on the short end of a 7–0 defeat.

below right: The Texas–Texas A&M game has been played 112 times, tied for the third-most in major college football history.

OFFICIAL PROGRAM
PRICE 25c

AUSTIN, TEXAS
NOV. 28, 1940

above: Freshman running back Earl Campbell led
the Longhorns to a 32–3 rout of the Aggies in 1974,
but A&M would get revenge the next two seasons
under former Texas assistant Emory Bellard.

opposite page: Kris Stockton's 29-yard field goal in
the final seconds negated an A&M comeback
and preserved a 26–24 upset of
the No. 6 Aggies in 1998.

The collapse of the Aggies' bonfire stack in 1999 killed 12 current or former students and drastically changed the tenor of the rivalry.

A&M players helped clear logs from the bonfire collapse. A week later they came back in the final quarter to beat the No. 7 Longhorns 20–16.

horns hadn't won at Kyle Field since 1923, so a group of concerned students solicited the help of local fortune-teller Madame Augusta Hipple, who advised them of an old Chinese tradition of burning red candles to overturn hexes. Texas rolled to a 23–0 victory, continuing a string that would see Texas win eight straight and 31 of the next 35 meetings between the teams.

Under Emory Bellard, who took the Aggie job in 1972 after successfully installing and dominating with the wishbone at Texas, the Aggies won back-to-back games in '75 and '76.

"I always had been on the Texas side of the fence, but when I went to A&M, there was no question about what side of the fence I was on then," Bellard said. "The thing I found out being on both sides of the fence is that each school has total respect for the other. Ninety-nine percent of the fans party together before the game, go their separate ways during the game, and after the game they party together again. I guarantee you, though, not a living one will ever tell you in a positive voice anything about the other."

That was particularly true when the Aggies, tired of living in Texas's shadow, made Jackie Sherrill the first million-dollar coach, luring him away from Pitt in 1982 with a deal that paid him $282,000 annually over six years. A&M was lambasted in the national media for paying such an exorbitant amount, but the Aggies got what they paid for. After a 49–7 loss to SMU in his first season, Sherrill made a promise. "We will get to the point where we will be very awesome. And it won't be very long. So all the people better get their licks in while they can."

Texas beat the Aggies 53–16 that year and 45–13 the next and when the teams met in Austin in 1984 the Longhorns, though they had slipped precipitously from an early No. 1 ranking, were still planning to easily dispatch the Aggies. A&M jumped to a 20–0 lead and routed the Longhorns 37–12. Until that game, A&M had only won back-to-back games in the series three times, and its longest series streak was three, from when Moran was coach.

The Aggies won six straight under Sherrill, and after he left under the cloud of an NCAA investigation, the Long-

horns beat A&M and new coach R. C. Slocum in their magical Cotton Bowl run of 1990. They then reverted back to form. A&M won the next four until the Aggies went on NCAA probation. An improved Texas program, buoyed by the formation of the Big 12, regained control.

Stafford tells a story about his recruitment by Sherrill that sums up the feelings between Texas and A&M during that period.

"He wanted me badly," said Stafford, a highly recruited quarterback out of Belton. "I don't know if he just wanted to take me away from somebody or he thought I could play for him. He sold my mom and the first sign of a good recruiter is get the mom at your hip."

Aggies President Ray Bowen grabs Bevo's reins during a 2002 visit to Royal-Texas Memorial Stadium.

Stafford, though, was noncommittal and he had scheduled visits to College Station and Austin on successive weekends. He had a good visit to A&M and Sherrill asked him one favor—not to commit while he was on the Texas campus. Stafford told him he would wait.

Texas Coach Fred Akers, though, was at his recruiting best. "Fred held up my jersey with my name on the back and I said, 'Fred, I'm coming,'" Stafford recalled. "All I asked him was just to keep it between him and me."

Stafford got in his pickup truck and headed back on the hourlong drive home. A message to call Sherrill was waiting.

Mack Brown gets doused after the 40–29 victory at Kyle Field in 2005 that capped the Longhorns' first unbeaten regular season since 1983.

"He said, 'I wanted to congratulate you on going to Texas—and I want you to know what it's going to be like to have 40 Aggies stomping your ass every year,'" Stafford recalled.

Stafford said Davis, then the Aggie coordinator, called him back to apologize. Davis does not recall the conversation.

In 1909, the Aggies began one of their most treasured traditions, when a group of students gathered around a burning trash heap in the days before their game with Texas. Over the years it grew larger and larger, reaching 109 feet in 1969, and only failed to burn once. In 1963, out of

respect for the recently assassinated President John F. Kennedy, the bonfire—and the one that Texas also burned before the game—was dismantled.

In the early morning hours of November 18, 1999, as former and current students swarmed the stack, wire holding the logs together snapped. The center pole also broke, sending the logs cascading to the side and trapping and crushing the workers.

By that afternoon, students, rescue workers, and members of the football team had removed all the victims. Eleven had died in the collapse. Another would die from his injuries within two days, giving a chilling total—twelve, just as in the Aggies' revered Twelfth Man tradition.

When news of the tragedy spread to Austin, the Longhorns organized blood drives and canceled their own Hex Rally, instead inviting Aggies and burning candles that featured the color both schools shared, white. The UT Tower was darkened and the band played "The Spirit of Aggieland." A week after the collapse, on the night the bonfire was to have burned, 50,000 people gathered at the site for a candlelight vigil. During its pregame performance, the Longhorn band carried A&M flags and played "Amazing Grace."

The Longhorns' entire trip to College Station was surreal. On the bus ride over one player had an epileptic seizure. Major Applewhite came down with a stomach virus. Pranksters called the rooms of Longhorn starters throughout the night, and when players gathered for their pregame meal, they were told none was available, forcing many of them to hurry to a nearby fast-food restaurant.

Texas led 16–6, but the emotional Aggies were not finished. Ja'Mar Toombs scored from 9 yards near the end of the third quarter and quarterback Randy McCown capped the comeback with a touchdown pass to Matt Bumgardner in the corner of the end zone. Linebacker Brian Gamble's recovery of a fumble by Applewhite, who had entered the game late in a vain attempt to rally the Longhorns, sealed the victory.

"We put our hearts and soul into this game," Gamble said. "I know God and those Aggies were looking down on us."

"We may not have had a bonfire this year," McCown said. "But there was a bonfire burning in our hearts today."

In 1915, when the rivalry resumed with conviviality and respect, the Longhorn alumni magazine foresaw a change in the rivalry. As noted in Maher and Bohls's book, *Long Live the Longhorns,* the *Alcalde* alumni magazine stated that "the football teams of these institutions have risen above the petty jealousies that used to characterize their movements at times, and have reached a point where they are willing to place sportsmanship above victory."

That time, if just for a brief moment, had at long last come.

Texas fans get their horns up—pinky and index fingers extended, thumb over middle and ring finger—as they sing "The Eyes of Texas" or "Texas Fight!"

Hook 'em Horns

It's got many meanings across the world: some that suggest you are calling a man a cuckold; some that suggest you have satanic ties; some that suggest you're trying to ward off evil; some that suggest you're an infielder reminding your teammates there are two outs.

To anyone who calls a particular color "burnt orange" instead of "rust," it means one thing.

"It's kind of like in *Batman,* when they put out the bat signal," said Anthony Hicks, a linebacker in the late 1990s, of the famed "Hook 'em Horns" hand signal. "It's one of those symbols you put in the sky: 'Calling all Horns. Time to rally.'"

In 1955, Harley Clark was the Longhorns' head cheerleader, a position he joked was second in importance in the state behind only the governorship. A friend of his, James Norton, had a buddy who was goofing around one day, doing shadow puppets, when he did the sign. Norton, thinking it was interesting, showed it to his friend Clark.

Clark tested it around campus, only to be told it was hokey. Unfazed, he decided he would do it at the end of a pep rally at Gregory Gym before the Texas Christian game and declare it the official Longhorn signal.

Aggies had been doing the "Gig 'em" hand gesture—basically a thumbs-up—for a quarter century, so Clark decided the Longhorns needed one.

"It's time we had a hand sign of our own," he informed the fans. "I want everybody to do this."

Shocked by his insolence, the administrators told him he was out of control. The students loved it. The students won out. A statue of Clark doing the sign now stands next to the Alumni Center and Royal-Texas Memorial Stadium

With President Bush in the White House the symbol has gotten worldwide exposure, not all of it positive. First daughter Jenna Bush flashed the sign when the Longhorn band passed the reviewing stand during the 2005 inauguration in Washington, D.C., which set the Norwegian press buzzing over a supposed satanic sign. In Russia, some saw it through their local interpretation—an indication that someone is an arrogant idiot.

Texas's opponents flash the sign with the fingers facing down. No interpretation of that is necessary.

Coach Mack Brown had seen the "Hook 'em" sign many times during his Saturdays watching college football as a kid and flashed it flawlessly when introduced as head coach in December 1997.

"I don't think I understood what it meant the first time," Brown said. "I've come to know that it's a culture. It's a passion. It's a way to communicate with fans across the country and in this state that care about this school. And until you understand that I don't think you really understand this place."

Brown jokes that in almost nine years at Texas, it's a reflex when he hears the piped-in "Eyes of Texas" in the elevator at the Moncrief-Neuhaus Athletic Complex.

"I throw the horns up without thinking about it," he said.

9

GREATEST MOMENTS

Maybe it came down to a second. An inch. A sliver of opportunity that presented itself for the briefest of moments—and was answered.

Maybe it was a day that made history. Or a day that recalled it. A great victory or a great escape.

Maybe it was moment that defined a team. Or a man. Or both.

Texas football has seen them all in its rich and glorious history. For a Texas fan, picking the greatest moment is like selecting one's favorite burnt-

Though Royal-Texas Memorial Stadium has undergone many renovations and even a name change, it's been the site of many of the greatest moments in Longhorn history.

orange sunset. While others fade, some remain, etched in the memory forever.

Chevigny does Rockne

October 6, 1934

Texas 7, Notre Dame 6, South Bend

Jack Chevigny didn't need to use his charisma and imagination and vast storytelling skills to spin a motivational tale for his Texas Longhorns; he could just tell them the truth.

Back in 1928, Chevigny was a halfback for Knute Rockne's 4–2 Notre Dame team, which found itself facing powerhouse Army at Yankee Stadium. Rockne, never one to shrink from the dramatic, delivered a pregame pep talk for the ages, calling on the Fighting Irish to dedicate their efforts to a deceased Irish All-American halfback named George Gipp.

Late in the game, the 193-pound Chevigny scored from the 1 on fourth down to put Notre Dame ahead to stay in a 12–6 victory, reputedly shouting, "That's one for the Gipper."

Six years later, Chevigny was on the other end of it as a first-year coach at Texas. Hired away from crosstown university St. Edwards, the 28-year-old inherited a schedule that included a home game against Notre Dame. The Irish were four years removed from the Rockne era and coming off a 3-5-1 season under "Hunk" Anderson, for whom

Chevigny, then a Notre Dame assistant, had been passed over.

Texas officials, worried that there would be a repeat of the Irish's 29-point rout in 1915, offered to cancel or postpone the game. Chevigny, sensing the possibility of a program-making win against a team that, while down, still carried the coast-to-coast cachet of Notre Dame, wouldn't have it.

After an opening-game victory at Texas Tech, the Longhorns received a sendoff from 6,000 fans at Gregory Gym and took an overnight train ride to Chicago, where they were met by sportswriters. Chevigny began sandbagging, telling them, "I think we will be lucky to hold them to five touchdowns," but that was all bluster. That Notre Dame team was coached by first-year coach Elmer Layden, the biggest and fastest of the famed Four Horsemen, who was still building a program that would result in a disputed national title in 1938. Though the Irish were led by a pair of All-Americans, center Jack Robinson and halfback George Melinkovich, they would finish only 6-3.

That didn't stop Chevigny from portraying the Irish as world-beaters and using a stirring pregame pep talk. Rather than retell the Gipper story, Chevigny borrowed a page from Rockne and bent the truth. Until it broke. Chevigny waxed passionately about Rockne, his mother, and his father, who he said was on his deathbed. Actually, Chevigny's fa-

ther was at the game, but the Longhorns were none the wiser.

The speech had the desired effect. "We were like a bunch of demons when we went out to play," reserve end and future Athletic Council chairman J. Neils Thompson would later say.

Texas kicked off to Melinkovich, who fumbled. Texas end Jack Gray recovered at the Ramblers' 18-yard line. Four plays later, halfback Bohn Hilliard burst through the middle of the Longhorn line for an 8-yard touchdown and a 7–0 lead. Texas's defense held up, and the Longhorns had helped put Southwest football on the national map. Governor-elect James V. Allred and an escort of fire engines greeted the Longhorns on their return, but the team had eaten some spoiled ice cream in Texarkana and spent much of the cele-bration vomiting over the sides of the trucks.

When World War II came, Chevigny enlisted in the Marines and took part in the invasion of Iwo Jima as a first lieutenant in the Fifth Division, which spearheaded the attack. Accounts differ, but on either the first or second day of the landings he was sharing a foxhole with former Minnesota All-American George Franck as shells rained down. Franck scurried to find better cover. A few minutes later a shell killed Chevigny.

After the war a story circulated that aboard the USS *Missouri* in Tokyo Bay in September 1945 a Japanese admiral signed the instrument of surrender using a gold pen that was inscribed: "To Jack Chevigny, an old Notre Damer who beat Notre Dame." The story has never been substantiated.

Jack Crain heads toward the goal line with the short pass that stunned Arkansas in 1939.

Favorite Bible Reverse

October 21, 1939
Texas 14, Arkansas 13, Austin

Texas Coach Dana X. Bible was hired in 1937 to restore the Longhorns' football fortunes, but after a combined 3-14-1 mark in his first two seasons, it became evident a drastic turnaround needed to happen.

That's where Jack Crain, a 5-foot-6 150-pounder from Class B Nocona who was only offered a one-year "make-good" scholarship, came in. If Crain, nicknamed the "Nocona Nugget," had one thing in excess, it was the ability to make a quick move.

Arkansas gave the fans every reason to expect a repeat of the 1938 game, in which it routed Texas 42–6, when it drove 91 yards on its possession for a 7-yard Kay Eakin touchdown. Milton Simington, a 225-pound guard, was wide with the extra point, but Arkansas led 6–0.

Texas took the lead later in the first quarter, when Crain ran down a punt that had sailed over his head, picked it up at the 10, and weaved his way down to the Arkansas 8. Three plays later R. B. Patrick dove over from the 1, Crain kicked the point after, and Texas led 7–6.

Arkansas nearly regained the lead in the third quarter when a pass interference call gave the Razorbacks a first down at the Texas 8, but Patrick dove on a fumbled lateral. Later, the Razorbacks, aided by an unnecessary roughness call on the Longhorns, drove to the 1, from where Eakin scored. Simington's kick made it 13–7 in favor of Arkansas.

The Razorbacks had dominated, and many in the crowd of 17,000 began to leave. Arkansas outgained the Longhorns 385 yards to 145 and had 19 first downs to Texas's 5. The Razorbacks enjoyed a huge edge in field position the entire game, so much so that Weldon Hart of the *Austin American* wrote, "If the goal line had been an electrical power line, every Texas lineman would have been electrocuted."

With a minute to play Floyd Lyons tried to pin Texas deep again by punting the ball out of bounds, but Patrick scooped it up on the sideline and returned it to the Arkansas 31. John Gill,

Crain, nicknamed the "Nocona Nugget" because of his hometown and diminutive stature, kicked the deciding extra point in the victory over the Razorbacks.

who entered the game at blocking back on the previous series, switched positions with Crain so Crain would be in a better position to catch the ball.

Patrick took the snap and fired a short pass into the right flat to Crain at the 33. As Gill blocked an Arkansas defender, Crain put a move on another and reversed field, finding a seam near the sideline and sprinting for the tying touchdown. With Patrick holding, Crain kicked the extra point that gave Texas a 14–13 lead.

After the kick the Longhorn fans stormed the field, drawing a 15-yard delay of game penalty. Patrick blasted the kickoff out of bounds at the Texas 44 with eight seconds left. Guy Gray dropped back to pass and scrambled, causing a few anxious moments before end Malcolm Kutner brought him down at the Texas 20.

"That was a pretty close shave," Bible said.

"Now you see why my hair is gray," Bible's wife told the *Austin Statesman,* "and D.X. is bald."

"That play and that victory changed our outlook—mine, the players', the student body's, and the ex students'," Bible told Lou Maysel in *Here Come the Texas Longhorns, Vol. 1.* "Things had been going pretty badly up until that game. The way was still long but we had tasted the fruits of victory and we were on our way."

"That was a turning point for Texas football," Kutner said. "Usually we would get beat every week and the student body didn't pay any attention to you. In that 1939 game, they said, 'Gosh, maybe we do have a football team.'"

The Impossible Catch

November 28, 1940
Texas 7, Texas A&M 0, Austin

Dana X. Bible didn't want any misunderstanding. At a pep rally the night before the Longhorns hosted the defending champion Texas A&M Aggies, he kept repeating the same thing—that the Aggies hadn't won in Austin since, well, never.

End Malcolm Kutner started buying into Bible's spiel, until later at the dorm he asked roommate and Texas quarterback Pete Layden if he thought they'd beat the Aggies.

"Hell no," Layden said, "but we'll get them next year."

Twenty-four hours later Layden was known as the man who threw the ball to Noble Doss for "The Impossible Catch"—the twisting, over-the-shoulder grab that made a liar out of Layden and spoilers out of the Longhorns.

Before the game, Bible recited the poem, "It Can Be Done," by Edgar Guest, which ended with this verse:

One play after Doss's catch, Pete Layden plunged
over from the 1-yard line for the only points
in the Longhorns' 7–0 upset of A&M.

Just start to sing as you tackle the thing
That "cannot be done," and you'll do it.

Texas came out passing and before the fourth play Noble Doss went back to the huddle and told Crain and Layden he thought he could get behind the man covering him, Aggies All-American John Kimbrough. Doss ran a down-and-out, and when he got a step on Kimbrough, Layden heaved it deep. Doss caught the ball over his shoulder and fell to the ground at the A&M 1. Layden dove over for a touchdown on the next play.

In the famous photo of the play, Doss's eyes are closed.

"I must have closed them after the catch," Doss later said.

The Longhorns didn't think one touchdown would hold up against the powerful Aggies, but they picked off five passes, including three by Doss, and kept turning the Aggies away. A&M didn't get past the Longhorns' 38-yard line in the second half. A&M's 20-game winning streak was over and the Rose Bowl, rumored to be ready to snap up the Aggies, instead took Nebraska.

After the game, Kimbrough, a gash on one cheek, told reporters, "No, it wasn't the best team we've played. SMU was better. But they beat the hell out of us, that's all. It looks like they did our thinking for us. And, man, I was so busy ducking and dodging I couldn't see anybody."

A story in the *Austin American* described an unhappy and "very drunk" A&M booster in the postgame press box grumbling, "Ain't right. Just ain't right. Was gonna spend my Christmas vacation in California—gonna see Rose Bowl game. Now whatama gonna do?"

The story continued, "He trailed off in a high-pitched note of inquiry, but nobody in the press box had any satisfactory answer to give him. They were too busy making the nation's telegraph wires sing with the fantastic news of the Texas Longhorns' 7–0 victory over the mighty Texas Aggies."

Noble Doss hauls in "The Impossible Catch" against A&M in 1940. Doss swore he only closed his eyes after he caught the ball.

"Right Where We Want 'em"

October 20, 1962
Texas 7, Arkansas 3, Austin

Johnny Treadwell wasn't known for speeches. Fact is, he wasn't much known for talking, period.

"Usually the first thing I heard from Johnny all day when we played," said fellow Longhorn linebacker Pat Culpepper, "was when he said right before kickoff, 'Let's go kick their ass.'"

Conceded Treadwell, "I always thought talking was a waste of time.

On a steamy October night, with Arkansas about to score from inside the Longhorn 10-yard line, the senior linebacker gave one of the most famous speeches in Texas history.

"We've got them right where we want 'em," he said in the huddle. "They have to come right at us."

This was the kind of drama the sellout crowd had come for. Expecting a huge crowd, Texas officials had 4,400 bleacher seats erected in the south end zone. Demand for seats had scalpers seeking up to $50 a ticket and Travis County Attorney Jerry Dellana said those selling tickets for profit ran the risk of a fine of up to $500. "We will prosecute," he said.

Arkansas was set to send the crowd home unhappy when, after an early field goal, the Razorbacks drove to a first-and-goal at the Longhorn 5 late in the third quarter. On first down, a sweep got the ball to the 2. The Razorbacks then sent fullback Danny Brabham into the middle for no gain. On third down, they tried Brabham again.

Marvin Kubin hit Brabham at the belt. Treadwell stacked him up head-on. Culpepper put his helmet on the ball. It popped loose and Joe Dixon recovered in the end zone.

"A linebacker is only as good as his line, as most backs are. If the line does its job, the poor back is naked as a jaybird," Treadwell said. "If you look at the picture, their line is all on the ground. There's nobody there, because my line put them there. Culpepper put a hat on the ball and I came over and got my picture taken."

Texas fumbled a few plays later and Treadwell had to stop Arkansas quarterback Johnny Moore on a fourth-and-goal sneak. Texas got the ball back and drove 90 yards in 20 plays, with halfback Tommy Ford scoring the winning touchdown with 36 seconds left.

The goal line tackle was captured in a classic photo in the *Austin American*. A week later, at the Longhorn Club meeting, coach Darrell Royal invoked the classic World War II photo taken by Joe Rosenthal at Iwo Jima.

"This," Royal said, "is our flag-raising at Mount Suribachi."

Treadwell kept a colorized version of the photo in his veterinary office until

*Johnny Treadwell (60) and Pat Culpepper (31)
stack up Arkansas fullback Danny Brabham.
Coach Darrell Royal called this shot
"our flag-raising at Mount Suribachi."*

he retired in early 2006 and it now hangs in his daughter's children's sporting apparel store in Austin.

Culpepper has a copy of the photo, too, and a card his wife got from an Arkansas guard when she ran into him at a meeting in Fort Worth.

"I missed that block on Pat," the card reads. It's signed by Jerry Jones, the Dallas Cowboys owner.

The Streak Lives

October 3, 1970
Texas 20, UCLA 17, Austin

Nothing seemed normal about the day the No. 13 Bruins came to town, seeking to end the Longhorns' 22-game winning streak. The game was interrupted several times when a small dog ran onto the field and had to be chased away, only to return. In the first quarter an Associated Press photographer got knocked down on the sideline by two players and broke his leg. In the stands Kathryn Hewlett, the 55-year-old wife of Texas academic counselor Lan Hewlett, suffered an apparent heart attack and died.

More to the point, the Longhorns' wishbone was stymied. Bruins Coach Tommy Prothro devised a plan to blitz outside linebackers and cornerbacks at the pitch, disrupting the option. The Longhorns also wasted numerous opportunities. Quarterback Eddie Phillips fumbled at the UCLA 5, ending one drive, and recovered his own drop at the 37 on another, forcing the Longhorns to try a field goal, which Happy Feller made from a then Southwest Conference record 55 yards. Early in the game he also pitched the ball to Billy Dale for an apparent touchdown, but it was ruled a forward lateral and the Longhorns had

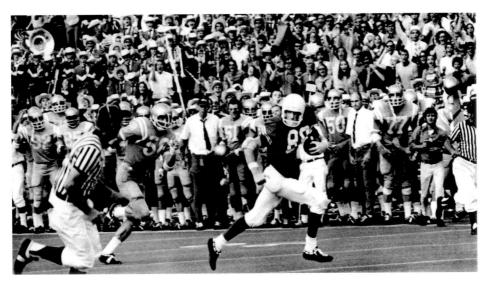

Cotton Speyrer sprints past a stunned UCLA bench on his way to the touchdown pass that kept the Longhorns' winning streak alive.

to settle for another field goal attempt, which was no good.

When the Bruins stopped the Longhorns at their own 12, ahead 17–13 with 2:27 left, the streak appeared over. The Longhorns got the ball back at their own 49 with 52 seconds left.

A sack and fumble out of bounds stopped the clock with 20 seconds left.

"We noticed in film work that they might be vulnerable if the tight end came across and the flanker went deep," Phillips said. "Sam Post, Ted Crossing" was the play. "On film their safety was biting on it but I think we had tried it three times in the game with no success."

They called it again, but this time with an unexpected twist from their tight end. "I think Tommy Woodard took it on himself to go 20 yards instead of 10 yards," Phillips said. "It was a little different view for the safety, and he did bite."

Phillips threw a perfect pass to split end Cotton Speyrer, who caught the ball at the 20 and sprinted in for a 45-yard touchdown with 12 seconds left.

"I just went for the ball—and the defenders did, too," Speyrer said. "I consider that a miracle."

On the sideline, coach Darrell Royal was so happy he jumped up and wrapped his arms and legs around tackle Bill Atessis.

Phillips was talking to reporters after the game when a man came up and

Speyrer's speed kept defenses honest. Without him in the 1971 Cotton Bowl, the Longhorns couldn't hurt Notre Dame deep.

stuck out his hand to Phillips. "You had me scared, there, Eddie," said James Street, who had won the first 20 games in the streak.

"You thought you were scared," Phillips cried. "I was scared, too."

Phillips said he still enjoys studying a photo taken from the Longhorn sideline of Speyrer running for the winning touchdown. "That's the greatest picture I've ever seen," Phillips said. "You look behind Cotton, across the field on their sideline and the expression on Prothro and everybody was amazing. It was just shock. That picture captured the essence of what happened."

Phillips said the Longhorns never discussed their close call, which would allow the winning string to reach 30 before Notre Dame snapped it in the Cotton Bowl.

"We didn't talk about the streak," Phillips said. "We thought it would go on forever."

Little Big Man

October 17, 1987
Texas 16, Arkansas 14, Little Rock

They said Tony Jones wouldn't go over the middle. They said his hands were suspect. They said he could make big plays and ruin small ones.

Then, in front of a frenzied crowd of 54,902 at War Memorial Stadium, he went over the middle against the most

*Tony Jones wasn't sure the officials would rule
his catch a touchdown after he took licks
from both Arkansas safeties.*

physical safety in college football and caught the game-winning pass for the first last-play victory in the history of University of Texas football.

"He'd been hit or miss," Coach David McWilliams said. "Afterward he didn't miss. I don't think I've ever seen one play change anybody's career like that. I always tell the young kids about that story."

Jones felt it, too. "At that moment, people finally recognized me as a football player," said the high school sprinter, who went on to have a nine-year professional career with the Houston Oilers and Atlanta Falcons. "It pretty much took my game to another level."

That moment never seemed likely, even as it unfolded. Texas went into the game planning to throw to halfback Eric Metcalf, who ended up catching a school-record 11 passes. The 5'7" Jones, meanwhile, didn't figure to stand up against the pounding of Arkansas safety Steve Atwater, who frequently drew him in the Razorbacks' cover two scheme.

On the first play of the game, Texas threw a wide receiver screen to Jones. Atwater wrapped him up.

"He came up and hit me in the chest," Jones recalled. "I was like 140 pounds. I thought it was funny. I said, 'Is that all you've got?' I had taken his best shot. Let's play."

No. 15 Arkansas led 14–10 with six minutes left in the game when the Longhorns, desperate, went for it on fourth and three at the Arkansas 14. Razorbacks noseguard Tony Cherico pressured Bret Stafford into an incompletion.

When the Longhorns got the ball back with 1:48 at their own 44 after a 12-yard punt return by Metcalf, Stafford threw to Darron Norris, who ran for 9 yards before fumbling.

Texas center Alan Champagne recovered.

"I don't know how he got over there but he did and dug it out," McWilliams said. "Otherwise the game would have been over."

"I had the ball," Atwater said. "There was no question about it. A Texas player jumped into the pile and grabbed it from me."

On fourth and 10 at the Arkansas 32, Stafford threw to Metcalf for a first down with 14 seconds left. An incompletion and illegal procedure penalty stopped the clock, allowing a quick sideline conference.

"It was like it was meant to be," Stafford said. "Too many things happened to get it right."

McWilliams remembers talking with offensive coordinator John Mize about what to call. "John and I were talking, 'We might throw this, we might throw that.' I looked at Bret and said, 'What do you think?' He said, 'If I roll right and throw back to Tony, I think I can get the ball back in there.' I didn't have any good ideas. I thought hell, he's the one who's got to do it. Let's go with it."

Metcalf lined up in the left slot and went outside, taking the linebacker with him. Jones headed toward the post. Stafford rolled left, looked off Atwater, and fired the ball.

"Steve hit him at the same time and I got a piece of the ball," Arkansas safety Anthoney Cooney said. "I got there about the same time the ball did."

Jones pinballed off Atwater and Cooney and fell to the turf.

"I knew I'd been hit hard," Jones said. "I looked up at the ref. Did I catch the ball? Did I hold on? Or drop it?"

The back judge didn't move his hands "Finally the side judge signaled touchdown," McWilliams said. "I don't know if I've ever been as happy to win the game. I jumped up. Then I looked over at the Arkansas sideline. There's [Arkansas Coach Ken] Hatfield, crouching down, head down, pulling on his cap. I felt sorry for him."

As Mark Rosner wrote in the *Austin American-Statesman,* "The Red Sea became the Dead Sea." Jones was hit again, this time by teammates, who joyously dogpiled him.

Asked almost two decades later what he remembered about the crowd reaction, Jones laughed.

"By the time I got up," Jones said, "the stadium was empty."

Steeler Roll Left

December 7, 1996
Texas 37, Nebraska 27, St. Louis

James Brown didn't come to the weekly Monday media luncheon and press conference looking to make headlines.

"I went," Brown said, "to see what I was going to have for lunch. Then I got tired of it."

What Brown got tired of was reporters asking him about being a three-touchdown underdog to Nebraska in the first Big 12 championship game at the TWA Dome in St. Louis.

"I had too much pride for that. I don't like people telling me I was going to lose. By the end of the day everyone had bombarded me with questions like, 'How does it feel to be expected to lose by three touchdowns?' and 'How does it feel to be going up against a power like Nebraska?'"

Said Brown, "I think we're going to win by three touchdowns."

To this day he doesn't think that was so outlandish. "I thought we matched up well. Nebraska liked to run eight-man fronts, play a lot of man-to-man," he said. "We had a good offense. We had three great backs in Shon [Mitchell], Ricky [Williams], and Priest [Holmes]. We had a great line; we sent four to the league. And with Mike Adams and Pat Fitzgerald, we had great receivers."

At practice that day Coach John Mackovic came over to his quarterback.

"He said, 'James, I hope you can back up what you said,'" Brown said. "I said, 'All right, let's go.' Later we had a meeting and [safety] Chris Carter got up and said, 'That's how I feel, too.' [Center] Dan Neil came to me and said, 'I'm glad you said that.'"

So were some Nebraska fans who thought that their Cornhuskers might be overconfident. They sent Brown a bouquet of funeral lilies with a card that read, "Thanks for keeping us focused."

"I thought they were from a girl who had seen me in a magazine," Brown said. "I was so wet behind the ears I didn't even know they were funeral flowers. I was like, 'Hey, I got flowers.' I put them in a vase and put them in my window."

Brown said he knew the Longhorns had a chance to fulfill his prophecy early in the game when he was tackled near the Nebraska sideline. "They helped me up," Brown said. "You'd have thought they'd be all bark and bite. They were real cordial, nice guys. I was like, 'Okay, well *we're* not nice guys.'"

Brown ended up throwing for 353 yards, but the second of his two interceptions led to a Nebraska field goal that gave the Cornhuskers a 27–23 lead with 10:11 left in the game. Four plays later Brown hit Wane McGarity with a 66-yard touchdown pass and after a defensive stop, the Longhorns got the ball back.

On fourth-and-inches at his own 28, Mackovic looked at his play list and chose the one with a blue star next to it—Steeler Roll Left. The Longhorns lined up with three tight ends, including one in front of the fullback, with Brown instructed to play fake to Priest Holmes and roll to his left and either run or hit tight end Pat Fitzgerald, who lined up in the backfield, short, or tight end Derek Lewis deeper.

"As soon as I got up to the line of scrimmage I knew my guy was coming up in a blitz," Lewis said. "What did we need? Two inches. I knew I was open at about three [inches]."

Lewis caught the ball and ran 61 yards, looking up at the giant video screen above the end zone to know when to cover up when the pursuit caught up to him. Holmes, who scored three touchdowns on an afternoon when neither Mitchell nor Williams could break 20 yards, scored the final touchdown one play later.

"I don't know what's going to happen," stunned Nebraska Coach Tom Osborne said after the game. "We were hoping to go to the Sugar Bowl and play Florida State. We hadn't thought about anything else."

Instead, the Cornhuskers went to the Orange Bowl, where they whipped Virginia Tech 41–21. Texas slipped into Nebraska's spot in the Bowl Alliance, but lost to Penn State 38–15 in the Fiesta Bowl.

facing page (top): James Brown decides which wide-open tight end he wants to throw to, Derek Lewis (82) or Pat Fitzgerald (81), against Nebraska.

facing page (bottom): Derek Lewis glances up at the big-screen video board at the TWA Dome to check the Cornhuskers' pursuit on his 61-yard catch and run.

"If it doesn't work it's really a dumb call," said Nebraska end Grant Wistrom. "But Coach Mackovic is a genius."

And Brown was a prophet, albeit a shy prophet. Years later, when people seem to recognize him and ask if he played football, he says yes—at Beaumont Westbrook. "And I leave it at that," he said.

"That taught me what the eyes of Texas really meant," Brown said of his big day in St. Louis. "A huge following wherever you go."

Rush to History

November 27, 1998

Texas 26, Texas A&M 24, Austin

Throughout his senior season, Ricky Williams dismissed each record he broke, saying he didn't pay much attention to statistics. "Except one," he'd say—how many yards he needed to pass former Pittsburgh star Tony Dorsett as the major college all-time career rusher.

Ask him that question any time, any day, and he'd have the answer, down to the yard.

On the day after Thanksgiving in 1998, the answer was 63.

Of course, there was a Reebok advertisement on a billboard above the Longhorn practice field that kept a running tally, as if Williams could forget.

"Our goal wasn't 63 yards," center Russell Gaskamp said after the game.

facing page (top):
Ricky Williams could always tell you how many yards he was away from Tony Dorsett's major college career rushing record. After this run, the answer was: zero.

facing page (bottom): Williams jukes behind the block of wide receiver Wane McGarity on his record-breaking run.

"Ricky could get 63 in his sleep. Our goal was to get 200 on them."

Williams felt the same way, stripping away any drama of facing the 13th-rated Aggie rushing defense. The week before he broke the record, he said, "If you have a job, and you get a Christmas bonus, you're not surprised when you get it because you knew you were going to get it."

Williams had put off a shot at being a surefire top five NFL draft pick the year before to take aim at the mark Dorsett set from 1973 to '76, and as he grew closer to Dorsett's once seemingly unbreakable mark of 6,082, the school turned the game into a celebration, inviting Dorsett and planning an elaborate ceremony that would also include former Heisman Trophy winner John David Crow of A&M and Earl Campbell of Texas.

Any suspense about the record was quickly shattered. On a first-quarter handoff from Major Applewhite, an iso play called "L King Zin 53," Williams broke up the middle, dodged one A&M defender, and slipped through the tackle of a third and raced to the end zone behind the block of receiver Wane McGarity, carrying an Aggie defensive back into the end zone to complete a 60-yard touchdown.

"All I wanted to do was go sit on the bench," Williams said of his first reaction to the record-breaking touchdown run. "I was so tired, I was exhausted. I couldn't breathe. All my teammates were

hugging me; I was trying to say 'help,' but I couldn't get it out."

Williams wasn't through, and it was partly his own fault. Two of his fumbles led directly to Aggies touchdowns as A&M came back from a 23–7 early fourth quarter deficit to take a 24–23 lead with 2:20 left.

Then the Longhorns, who had relied on Williams all season to carry them, bailed him out. With Applewhite passing, including two key passes for third-down conversions to tight end Derek Lewis and wide receiver Bryan White, they moved 70 yards in 11 plays. Kris Stockton kicked his fourth field goal, from 24 yards out, with five seconds left, to save the victory.

Williams finished with 259 yards against the Aggies, giving him 6,279 for his career. The record that took 22 years to break, however, lasted only one more year, when Wisconsin's Ron Dayne reached 6,397.

"Ricky is the best player I have ever seen," Mack Brown said after the game. "I think he is one of the best, if not the best, college football player ever."

Texas players wore Cole Pittman's initials on their helmets to honor their fallen teammate.

44 for 44

September 8, 2001
Texas 44, North Carolina 14, Austin

Mack Brown held the telephone in his hand and wished he could be anywhere else in the world.

Cole Pittman was on his way back for spring practice when he was killed in a one-car crash in East Texas in February 2001.

It was the afternoon of February 26, 2001, and the father of one of his players was at the other end of the line saying, "Tell me my boy is with you. Tell me he's there."

Brown could tell Marc Pittman no such thing. Cole Pittman, returning earlier that morning from his home in Shreveport, Louisiana, to Austin for the first day of spring football practice, apparently fell asleep down a long stretch of two-lane highway near Franklin in East Texas. The junior defensive tackle's pickup veered off the road and flipped, landing upside down in a dry creek bed, killing him. He had turned 22 a month earlier.

Texas did several things to honor Pittman's memory. They had a sticker with his initials "CP" placed on the back of their helmets. They put Plexiglas over his locker, leaving it exactly as he had left it. They scheduled a day to honor him, co-incidentally on the same afternoon Coach Mack Brown would be facing his former team, the North Carolina Tar Heels.

University Federal Credit Union

TEXAS 0:23 UMC
44 TIME OUTS LEFT 2 14

DOWN 2

#21 RODERICK BABERS
JUNIOR CB 2L
5'10" 183 lb
...SSION, TX
LAMAR H.S.

TO GO 10

BALL ON 35

QTR 4

Fairtron

When Major Applewhite
took a knee instead of
holding for the extra point
after the Longhorns' final
touchdown, a chill went
through the crowd.

179

GREATEST MOMENTS

Marc, Chase, and
Judy Pittman are flanked
by Mack Brown and his
wife Sally as they watch
a scoreboard tribute to
Cole Pittman.

Before the game the Longhorns presented Pittman's parents, Marc and Judy, and his younger brother Chase—who in the locker room after the game would commit to play at Texas—a scrapbook, a framed jersey, and a stadium-full of hugs.

The game was a Texas rout from the beginning, with many of Pittman's clos-

est friends playing key roles. End Cory Redding, who would touch his finger to the CP sticker on his helmet and point to the sky after big games, dropped in a zone blitz, picked off a pass, and returned it for a touchdown. With the Longhorns up 38–14 late in the game, linebacker Reed Boyd, a hunting buddy who'd come to Texas in the same recruiting class as Pittman, intercepted a pass. Texas drove down and Brett Robin, another close friend, scored with thirty-six seconds left.

On the sideline, backup quarterback Chance Mock looked at the scoreboard. Mock, one of Cole Pittman's closest friends, who wore his old hunting jacket and called Pittman's parents every night at 9:30, just as Cole had done, pointed out the score to Brown. Brown called for Applewhite and told him to take a knee.

Texas lined up with Major Applewhite behind center. At the snap, he bent down. Slowly word spread through the crowd why he'd done it, and they began pointing to the scoreboard.

Under "Texas" was a "44."

"That's Cole's number," tackle Mike Williams said. "Divine power. It had to be."

The fans around the Pittmans began holding their hands up, four fingers on each extended. "I promise you, when 44 hit the board, I knew they'd take a knee," Marc Pittman, Cole's father, said after being given the game ball. "God was here in a mighty way."

"When Major took that knee, that was the probably the coolest thing I'd ever been around," said kicker Dusty Mangum, who would make the game-winning kick at the 2005 Rose Bowl. "I've been a part of some pretty historic moments in Texas football, but that was the coolest."

"The only way it could have been better," cornerback Quentin Jammer said after the game, "was if Cole was still with us."

"You Get to Be the Hero"
January 1, 2005
Texas 38, Michigan 37, Rose Bowl

When Dusty Mangum was an 11-year-old in Mesquite, Texas, getting his first taste of select team soccer, he knew he had to get every edge he could. So he began visualizing everything about the game. Where he got the ball. Who was marking him. What he would do with the ball.

The practice carried with him, as he earned second-team All-District honors as a placekicker at Mesquite High School, as he became a walk-on at Texas, as he won the starting job as a freshman, as he missed three of four field goals as a sophomore at home against Oklahoma State, and as he kicked 42- and 52-yarders to beat A&M on Senior Day 2005.

So when he and the Longhorns headed to Pasadena, California, to play in the school's first-ever Rose Bowl in his final collegiate game, he imagined two scenarios. In one, he kicked five field goals, including the game-winner, as Texas won and he was named game

MVP. "That would have been nice," Mangum laughed.

In the second, he didn't attempt a field goal until the final seconds and then drilled the game-winner. That one was nicer. It actually happened. "It's amazing how well that works," Mangum said.

When Garrett Rivas connected on his third field goal of the night, from 42 yards, to put Michigan up 37–35 with 3:04 left, Mangum turned away and said quietly, "Lord if it comes down to me, why not? Let's do it."

Mangum watched the game. He watched the clock. Defensive tackle Larry Dibbles tried to tell him a joke. Mangum waved him off. Dibbles understood.

After Cedric Benson gained one yard on second-and-11 to put the ball on the left hash, Mangum knew he was on. He started jogging on the field but coach Mack Brown waved him back. Looking his senior in the eye, Brown smiled and said, "You're the luckiest person in the world. You get to be the hero in the Rose Bowl. Now they're going to call two timeouts. Don't worry. You'll get your chance." Then he slapped Mangum on the helmet, and the loneliest man among almost 105,000 people in Arroyo Seco ran out with a smile.

During the first timeout, Mangum hummed a melody, Hoobastank's "Just One." Lost on him at the time were the lyrics,

Just one chance is all I ever wanted
Just one time I'd like to win the game.

"I didn't even know those were the lyrics," Mangum said. "I was just singing it because it was a good tune and it was the last one I'd heard on my iPod before we came out of the locker room."

Mangum stood off by himself, alternately staring at the ground and the goalposts. When the officials whistled the ball back in play, he stood at Tony Jeffrey's hold and took three steps back and two to his left. He flexed his kicking foot and shook his right arm to relax, a habit he'd inexplicably picked up a year before. He nodded at Jeffrey, who turned to take the snap.

When Nicky Schroeder delivered the ball, Mangum strode forward and put his instep into the ball. He swore he'd hit it true, solid, and perfect. "I'd crushed the thing," Mangum recalls. "It was gorgeous. When I looked up the rotation had changed, but I saw it was still going straight, through the uprights. I'd seen enough good field goals. I ran off before it had even gone through. Let's celebrate."

Not everyone in the Longhorn faction shared the feeling. Michigan safety Ernest Shazor, crashing around left end, and linebacker Prescott Burgess, leaping up the middle, stuck their hands up but the ball spun past their fingertips, over the crossbar, and between the posts.

Dusty Mangum kicks the field goal against Michigan that gave the Longhorns a victory in their first-ever BCS game.

pantheon of Longhorn football heroes.

Mangum became an instant celebrity. He had an autograph session at the University Co-Op, and people who a week earlier couldn't have picked him out of a lineup stood twenty-deep for his signature.

"It was like my Rudy moment, being a walk-on and ending up where I did," Mangum said.

Mangum's mother put the black Copa Mundial shoe with the Adidas logo blacked out with a Sharpie—Texas, after all, is a Nike school—with a photo of the kick and encased both in a shadow box as a reminder, not that Mangum could ever forget what happened that crisp January night.

A year and three days later, he sat in the stands at the Rose Bowl and watched his former team win a national championship. He waited outside the tunnel from the locker room to the buses to visit with his former teammates and congratulate them. "Wish you could have been playing in the game with us," they told him. "You started this last year with your kick."

Mangum gets warm at the memory. "We started it with the Rose Bowl win," he says. "We really did."

Texas had won its first-ever Bowl Championship Series game and Mangum was the hero.

Punter Taylor Landin met Mangum as he sprinted off, arms upraised, and lifted him. He told Mangum to tell the media when they came up with their microphones, as they were certain to do, that he was going to Disneyland. "I'm going to Disneyland," Mangum cried gleefully. In truth he was going someplace more exclusive, straight into the

Before games the field is a blur of spirit groups showing their pride, from the Texas Cowboys firing Smokey to the Longhorn Band unfurling a giant state flag to the cheerleaders running across the field with flags.

10

EARL AND RICKY

Tim Campbell describes the work he and his brothers did in the rose fields of Tyler four decades ago in a very matter of fact manner. It's easier now. Those days are behind him, and they no longer sweat him dry or cramp his fingers.

"We'd get up at five in the morning, eat breakfast and when daylight hit we were out in the fields and worked until three," he said. "It was kind of like if

Pose look familiar?
Earl Campbell flashes his formidable stiff arm
as he cuts behind a block by Rick Ingraham.

you have a stick in the ground, and you take a knife and split the stick. Then you stick another stick in the eye and wrap it up. That's what we did, all day, sometimes as many as two thousand times. If that eye lived, you had a rose."

In its heyday, Tyler produced millions of roses, which were shipped around the country, earning the small East Texas city the title of "Rose Capital of the World."

Tyler only produced one Earl Campbell. That was enough.

Before Campbell finished his Longhorn career in 1977, he would set school records for single-season and career rushing yardage, career rushing touchdowns, and shredded tearaway jerseys. Running with high knees, low shoulder pads, and one of football's fiercest stiff-

Campbell and his mother Ann celebrate after he became Texas's first Heisman Trophy winner.

arms, Campbell became the first Longhorn to win the Heisman Trophy and have his number, 20, retired.

As Chicago Bulls star Michael Jordan "posterized" hundreds of luckless defenders with his repertoire of slam dunks, Campbell did the same to defensive backs. There is a classic photo taken by Austin photographer Tom Lankes of Campbell apparently steamrolling a Southern Methodist cornerback, who's flat on his back with his arms slightly upraised, as if he's about to go into convulsions. It was such a compelling shot it became a poster. A very popular poster.

"It was in everybody's freakin' dorm room," said Sid Greehey.

One hangs on the wall of the offices of Greehey & Co, Ltd., in San Antonio. Greehey is the company president. He also was an SMU defensive back. That SMU defensive back.

"Anyone who knows anything about physics knows I wasn't run over," Greehey said, and in fact, Campbell is two feet over Greehey and had just slipped a diving ankle tackle. The photo, though, captured a moment that doesn't tell the full story.

"People bring that up to me all the time," Greehey said. "I even got Earl to sign a copy of it. He signed, 'That poor kid. Peace & Love, Earl.'"

There was love in the way Campbell ran, for full, snot-bubbling contact, but as such very little peace.

"There are a lot worse things to be

known for," said former Longhorn teammate Rick Ingraham, "than being run over by Earl Campbell."

Except, of course, if you're a Texas fan—then there's the grim and at one time entirely possible specter of being run over by an Earl Campbell wearing the crimson and cream of Oklahoma.

"The recruiting was crazy. Every school you can imagine had some kind of contact and in any way you can imagine," Tim Campbell said. "It wasn't anything to come home and see a coach there. One day it was Coach [Barry] Switzer. The next it was Coach Royal. The next it was Coach [Grant] Teaff."

When Royal visited, he told Earl that the only deal he was offering was a scholarship and the opportunity that went with it. Campbell insisted that was all he wanted: "I hope you don't think Earl Campbell is for sale, because I am not," he told Royal. "My people were bought and sold when they didn't have a choice. Now I have a choice and I'm not for sale."

Longhorn Assistant Coach Ken Dabbs, who lived for almost two weeks at the local Ramada Inn while trying to woo Campbell, finally won an oral commitment, but Campbell also wanted to honor his promises to visit Switzer at Oklahoma, Teaff at Baylor, and Bill Yeoman at Houston. It came down to Texas and Oklahoma, and Campbell whittled it down to one deciding factor.

The night before signing day, Camp-

His bladder is credited with guiding Campbell to Texas over Oklahoma.

bell prayed. He recalled the entreaty, for author Paddy Joe Miller in his authorized biography, *The Tyler Rose.*

"God, if it's your will that I should attend the University of Texas, then I'll get up during the night to pee. If not, if I sleep through the night, then I'll know your choice for me will be the University of Oklahoma."

Score one for the size of Campbell's bladder. The next day he signed with Texas.

As a child, Campbell didn't consider football his ticket out of the cycle of poverty he was born into, the sixth of eleven children of B.C. and Ann Campbell. When B.C. died of kidney and heart problems just weeks after Earl's eleventh birthday, though, Earl began to use football as an outlet for his feelings of loss and abandonment.

"I remember Mom sat us down and told us she'd feed us, she'd clothe us, but she would not come to jail to get us,"

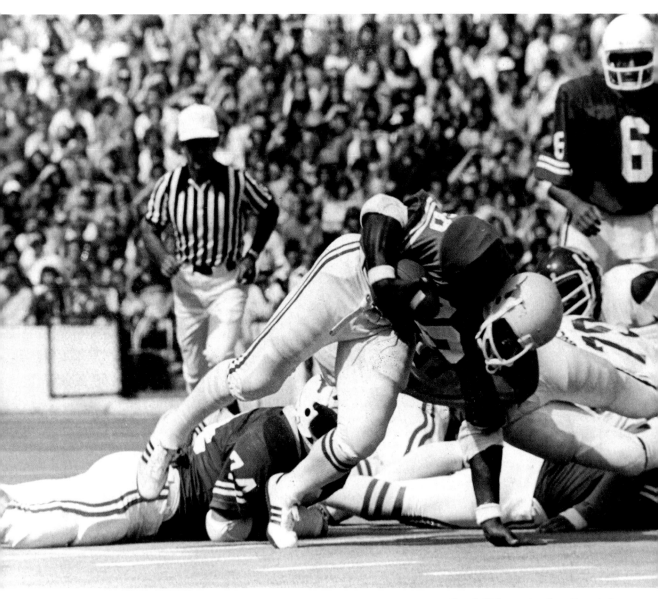

*Campbell's low center of gravity made it
difficult for one tackler to bring him down,
as the Sooners found out in 1977.*

brother Tim said. "That's why we never got in trouble. We knew Mom meant it."

That doesn't mean they didn't sometimes push the envelope. When Earl was in eighth grade, knowing Ann didn't want to risk injuries to her boys, he and his younger twin brothers, Tim and Steve, forged each other permission slips to play tackle football. Though he nearly didn't play football his sophomore year at John Tyler because he was no longer playing for his revered junior high coach Lawrence LaCroix, who had become a father figure, he talked Tyler Coach Corky Nelson into a second chance.

Campbell played linebacker and tailback his junior year and became the focal point of the Lions' offense as a senior. In the second round of the state playoffs against Conroe, he missed most of the second and third quarters with a concussion, but put himself in the game on the Lions' last drive, carrying on all but one play and scoring the winning touchdown. Tyler went on to win the 5A state title with a 21–14 victory over Austin Reagan at the Astrodome.

As a freshman at Texas, Campbell split time with Roosevelt Leaks, coming off a serious knee injury, as a wishbone fullback. The position fit his power but didn't take full advantage of his often overlooked speed. Ingraham, a guard who came to Texas in the same recruiting class in the fall of 1974 and who would later become one of Campbell's best blockers and even better friends, re-called him running with Raymond Clayborn and Alfred Jackson and other fleet Longhorns, and more than holding his own. "It was like Secretariat with a bunch of mules," Ingraham recalled. "People always asked, 'How fast is Earl?' As fast as he needs to be."

Working in tandem with quarterback Marty Akins, Campbell blossomed as a sophomore. A late-season knee injury to Akins and a loss to A&M relegated the Longhorns to the Astro-Bluebonnet Bowl, where Earl capped a 1,118-yard season by earning game offensive MVP honors while Tim blocked a punt and earned the defensive award. "I would like to put in a vote for Ann Campbell," Royal said of his MVP preference.

Campbell's junior season, thought to be his breakout year, got off to a bad start when he pulled a hamstring in spring football. It bothered him all summer and through most of the fall, and he played healthy in only one game, gaining 131 yards on 32 carries in a season finale victory over Arkansas, Royal's final game.

"He thought about quitting and he's not a quitter, that's how bad it got," Ingraham said of Campbell's psyche. "He felt he had let down everybody. It was a bad period. He'd never been hurt. Superman never gets hurt. He was probably weighing 240, 250. Earl didn't have the conditioning to play at that weight."

Ingraham said Campbell was also overwhelmed by the self-imposed pres-

A switch from wishbone fullback to I-formation tailback allowed Campbell to pound defenses inside and outrun them to the corner.

sure he felt to take care of his mother and his family.

"He was worried about the obligations he'd made, all the promises like, 'I'm going to buy my mom a house when I go pro,'" Ingraham said. "The great thing about Earl, though, is as bad and dark as it had been, he could always see the light."

New Coach Fred Akers made sure he shined it, too, calling him into his office and referring to him as "Mister Campbell," a sign of respect he learned from a coach during his playing days at Arkansas. Akers set down the rules. First of all, he told Campbell he could not play at his current weight, 246 pounds.

"I told him we would hand it to him, pitch it to him, throw it to him," Akers said. "To do that, he needed to lose 25 pounds. He said, 'I haven't weighed that much since my sophomore year in high school. How do I do that?' You need to watch what you drink and eat and we'll get you with Frank Medina."

Medina, the Longhorn trainer, devised a series of early morning workouts that whipped Campbell into shape. A change in the offense, which would move him from fullback to tailback and allow him to use his speed and power to turn the corner, dovetailed with his skills.

"We got a lot smarter when we pitched it to Earl twenty to thirty times a game instead of handing off to him a yard behind the quarterback," Ingraham

said. "And with Lam and Alfred at wide receiver we always had a soft corner."

Alfred Jackson was at one receiver; Lam Jones, who won an Olympic gold medal in the 400-meter relay in 1976 after his senior year at Lampassas High School, the other. Add to that a stout defense and a superlative kicking game, and the makings were there for Campbell to be a Heisman Trophy candidate.

Whatever that was.

One day during his sessions with Medina he read an article that talked about Tony Dorsett winning the 1976 Heisman and that mentioned the top candidates for the 1977 award. Campbell's name was not among them. He asked Medina what the Heisman Trophy was.

"It goes to the greatest player in America," Medina said.

Earl pondered the answer. "Next year," he said, "I'm going to win the Heisman Trophy."

Campbell's simplistic understanding of things delighted his teammates.

"Earl didn't grow up reading about Paul Hornung and the other Heisman greats," Ingraham said. "He didn't even have a television set. All that stuff was new to him. That's how supremely naive Earl was, so clean, so uncorrupted about those things. It was fun to teach him things."

Campbell started slowly, gaining only 87 yards on 17 carries in an opening game blowout of Boston College, but had 156 the following game against Virginia and then first got on the radar with a 131-yard, four-touchdown day against Rice.

He didn't yet have a high-profile game and got one the following week against Oklahoma, but his halfback pass on the second play of the game was intercepted. Still he ran for 124 yards as the Longhorns won.

Campbell's march to the Heisman appeared to hit a snag against Baylor, which held him down in the first quarter to under a yard a carry. When Campbell came back to huddle after one no gain, Ingraham didn't look up. "Heisman my ass," was all he said.

"I think he broke a sixty-yarder on the next play," Ingraham said.

"We smoked them pretty good," Campbell said.

With a high fever left over from an attack of tonsillitis, he ran 173 yards against Houston. Against Texas A&M, McEachern threw Campbell a rare screen pass that went for a touchdown—one of only five passes Campbell caught his senior season. Campbell set a personal best with 222 yards and three touchdowns and Texas blew out the Aggies to finish the regular season unbeaten. Campbell ended up with a then-conference record 1,744 yards and 19 touchdowns, which led the nation.

A large Texas delegation attended the Heisman Trophy ceremony and a limo was sent to ferry Campbell to the awards

facing page: Campbell's career ended on a down note when the Longhorns lost to Notre Dame in the Cotton Bowl despite his 116-yard day.

dinner. He put the rest of the group in the limo, sent it on its way, and instead hailed a cab with longtime friend Louis Murillo. Since his father's funeral, Campbell had always hated riding in limos.

"He always said it looked like a hearse," Murillo said. "He was always afraid of limos and needles."

Campbell won the Heisman Trophy with 1,547 points, 735 more than runner-up Terry Miller of Oklahoma State.

"When I was a kid and got in trouble, I'd always say, 'Mom, I'm in trouble,'" Campbell said as he got the trophy at the Downtown Athletic Club. "Well, Mom, I'm in trouble."

Campbell then thanked his coaches and teammates, talked of their love for each other, and then said, "I will do everything in my power to represent the Heisman Trophy the way it should be represented."

One copy of the trophy went to Tyler, where Ann Campbell still refers to it as "my Heisman." The other went to a trophy case in the T-Room at Belmont Hall, where only lettermen get to see it. Yet it wasn't forgotten.

After Campbell, every big-name running back that signed with Texas did so with expectations of giving the Longhorns a bookend Heisman. Edwin Simmons showed flashes as a freshman but his knees never let him achieve greatness. Charles Hunter announced as a redshirt freshman in 1985 that his goal was to run

for 2,000 yards. Told that would guarantee a Heisman, he just nodded. Eric Metcalf was the most elusive player of his time, but the Longhorns could never figure out how to use him.

In February 1995, Texas won a recruiting battle for a squarely built, dreadlocked, part-time baseball player out of San Diego. Southern California wanted him as a linebacker. Texas wanted him as a running back.

What Texas got was an introspective manchild, who said what was on his mind, and at times embraced the attention, once making his mother and sister wait for an hour while he signed almost 200 autographs after a game. At other times he pushed that spotlight away, frequently doing interviews wearing his helmet and reflective visor and once wrapping his right hand in tape so he could have a visible reason for not signing autographs.

The Longhorns got the best at what he did, a guy who could lead by example but who also posted a saying on his apartment refrigerator that read, "Don't follow me, I may not lead. Don't lead me, I may not follow. Just walk next to me and be my friend."

They got a player who would work hard to get in shape and then eat a dozen doughnuts as a reward; a baseball outfielder who called baseball his love but thankfully, for Longhorn fans, couldn't hit the breaking ball. They got a runner who seemed indestructible.

In fifth grade he fell on a broken vase, seriously lacerating his thigh. When his mother arrived in near panic, he smiled at her and said, "Mom, the paramedic gave me some gum!"

A few months later he got hit by a car

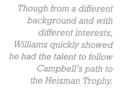

Though from a different background and with different interests, Williams quickly showed he had the talent to follow Campbell's path to the Heisman Trophy.

going 30 mph and walked away with broken ribs and a bruised thigh. "Unbelievable," said the attending physician. In college he didn't miss a game.

They got a free spirit who loved reggae, pierced his ears, nose, and tongue and had a Mighty Mouse tattoo on one bicep and barbed wire on the other. A dreamer who, as a high school junior, openly yearned for the twenty-room mansion and Lamborghinis that NFL millions could bring but when he had a chance to turn pro after his junior season came back to school—and then bummed a twenty off his mom.

They got a gamer who loved to compete at everything, but who would later walk away from football in his prime.

"On the field, Ricky used to keep score," linebacker Anthony Hicks remembered of the Longhorn practices. "Who outdid who. We'd make it into a competition, me and him. We'd go against each other in pass [drills], and there were times I covered him man to man. If I beat him up or he tried to make a move and I wrapped him up, it was my point. If he blew by me on a pattern and made a catch, he'd get a point. For the first couple of years, Ricky would win. The last couple of years I caught up with his tricks, it was more even."

Even if Hicks figured out Williams's moves, few others did. Williams played fullback his first two seasons while junior college transfer Shon Mitchell started

Williams's dreadlocks grew to be his trademark. A popular T-shirt during his senior season featured a dreadlocked Heisman Trophy.

The UT Tower is lit with Williams's jersey number to celebrate his Heisman Trophy.

*Williams, fresh off his Heisman Trophy acceptance,
strikes a pose in the 38–11 victory over
Mississippi State in the Cotton Bowl.*

at halfback. In the Longhorns' split-back multiple pro offense the two positions were not significantly different. In his Longhorn debut at Hawaii he carried 10 times for 96 yards, broke a 65-yard touchdown run, and caught one pass for 48 yards, giving a taste of his versatility. Williams finished with 990 yards, breaking Campbell's freshman rushing record, and with quarterback James Brown hobbled with an ankle sprain, carried the Longhorn offensive load with 163 yards and two scores in a 16–6 victory at Texas A&M that earned the Longhorns the final Southwest Conference title.

After a solid sophomore year, in which he led the Longhorns with 1,272 yards rushing, Williams had a breakthrough junior season. Despite an inexperienced group of receivers that allowed opponents to stack the line, and a defense that often forced the Longhorns to play from behind, Williams had seven

games of at least 200 yards in an eight-week span. He finished with 1,893 yards and 25 touchdowns, both school records, won Big 12 offensive player of the year honors and the Doak Walker Award as the best running back in the country.

At the Walker Award ceremony, the finalists were given copies of a book about Walker. Williams read it, and was intrigued that Walker also played baseball. The two became friends.

Williams had a decision to make. Texas finished 4–7, had a new coach in Mack Brown, and was breaking in a new quarterback. Williams was projected as a likely top 5 pick in the 1998 NFL Draft, a position that would have likely commanded a signing bonus of at least $6 million. He had filled out the necessary paperwork. All he had to do was load the fax machine and dial.

At his January 9 press conference, Williams was at his teasing best. He

Williams could run over defenders, but he could also beat them to the pylon, as he did against UCLA in 1998.

talked of reasons to stay. He spoke convincingly of reasons to go. He went back and forth, finally saying, "and that's why I'll be back . . ." as the anxious staffers and fans gathered on the ninth floor of Bellmont Hall erupted in cheers.

"We have just had a successful recruiting class," Brown said after the excitement died down. "This is our first signee. He's the best football player in the country returning next year."

Later Williams said he appreciated the thanks he got from Longhorn fans. "They don't understand, because I didn't do them a favor," he said. "I did it for myself."

At the Walker Award dinner, Williams had met Tony Dorsett, the former Pittsburgh halfback and Heisman winner who held the NCAA Division I-A career rushing record. They shook hands and made small talk, including some about the record. To break Dorsett's mark of 6,082 yards, Williams would have to average 160.7 yards a game, about 12 fewer than he did his junior season.

When starting quarterback Richard Walton broke his finger against UCLA, it meant redshirt freshman Major Applewhite would get the start the following week at No. 5 Kansas State. Daring Applewhite to pass, the Wildcats stuffed Williams, holding him to 43 yards on 25 carries.

"They were yelling, 'You're all hype' and 'Ricky who?'" Williams said after the game. "One guy yelled, 'My daughter's run for more yards than you.' But hopefully I can bounce back."

Williams did, in a big way. The following week against Rice he ran for a school-record 6 touchdowns and 318 yards, 24 short of the school record of 342 set by Roosevelt Leaks against Southern Methodist in 1973. Williams just had to be patient. On October 3, in a 54–33 home victory over Iowa State, he got 350.

Three yards short, he approached Brown on the sideline in the fourth quarter asking back in. Brown told him he had one play. He took two, breaking the mark on a 9-yard sweep.

"When I first got to the University of Texas, I was looking through the media guide, and that record was one I never thought I'd have a chance to break," Williams said. "So it was one I was excited to break."

Williams also dedicated the performance to Doak Walker, who had passed away a week earlier from complications stemming from a skiing accident that had left him paralyzed. Williams wore a decal with Walker's number, 37, on his helmet but decided the next week to do one better when the Longhorns played Oklahoma at the Cotton Bowl, Walker's home field at SMU. He got permission from the Big 12 and NCAA to wear No. 37, and he responded with a 139-yard day. After the game, he tearfully met Walker's widow, Skeeter, and her family outside the locker room and gave them

*John David Crow and
Tony Dorsett help Williams
commemorate his record-
setting day against A&M.*

199

EARL AND RICKY

the game jersey, apologizing for the blood and sweat stains.

After his three touchdown runs—including a 78-yarder called back by a holding penalty—he pointed two fingers toward the sky and said, "This is for you, Doak."

Williams kept up the pace with 259 yards against Baylor and then sewed up the award in the minds of many voters when his 37-carry, 150-yard performance at No. 7 Nebraska grounded the Longhorns in a 20–16 upset that ended the Cornhuskers' NCAA-leading 47-game home winning streak.

Three years earlier, as a freshman at Texas, he had selected the e-mail address Heisman@mail.utexas.edu. Now he was

a shoo-in to get the award, so much so that he said a week before the ceremony, "I'm sure I'll be nervous making that speech. I'll have to make sure I thank all the people I'm supposed to. Otherwise, I'll have an answering machine full of nasty messages."

Williams was a runaway winner of the Heisman, a victory made sweeter because it came on the 50th anniversary of Walker's Heisman. His selection set a record for highest percentage of points (43 percent) and he received the second highest of first-place votes, with his 714 accounting for 77.6 percent, which trailed only the 80.5 percent of the 1993 winner Charlie Ward of Florida State.

"I wasn't nervous until I walked into

the Heisman room, and then I was just overwhelmed," Williams said. "When it came to the announcement, my heart was beating so fast, and I was so nervous. It was a relief to hear my name called."

He thanked everybody, from Walker to his coach and teammates to his mother, Sandy, who raised three children as a single parent.

Earl Campbell, who had joined the former Heisman winners at the ceremony, congratulated Williams. "When he was a freshman, I thought I was looking at my son," Campbell said at the ceremony. "He walked and moved like me. . . . I think he's the greatest. And he's part of a heckuva fraternity."

In recent years, both Campbell and Williams have struggled. Back surgery that was expected to ease some of the pain from the pounding Campbell accumulated in a nine-year Hall of Fame ca-

reer with the Houston Oilers and New Orleans Saints hasn't had the desired effects and he is still in near constant pain, rarely making public appearances. Teammates often call to see how he's doing. Sometimes he answers. He rarely calls back.

Said Ingraham, "He walks slow when he's healthy. When he isn't, he doesn't walk at all."

Williams battled his own set of problems. Unlike Campbell, who would just as soon run through a defender as around them, sticking his helmet into another player's chest was never Williams's muse. New Orleans Coach Mike Ditka heaped pressure on Williams, trading his entire set of 1999 draft picks and two more in 2000, including the No. 1 pick, to move up seven spots to No. 5 in the first round to draft Williams. After the pick, Ditka donned a dreadlocked wig, sat puffing a

When Williams walked off the field after his 150-yard performance at Nebraska the Cornhusker fans chanted, "Heisman, Heisman."

HEISMAN ROOM

Texas's two Heisman Trophy winners are the only Longhorn football players to have their numbers retired.

201

EARL AND RICKY

cigar, and told reporters, "We did the thing that this organization thought would make us the best the fastest. The future is now. It's not the year 2002, it's now."

Williams, though, couldn't live up to those expectations and, saddled with a contract he had pursued that would pay him mainly with incentives, instigated a trade to Miami, where he appeared renewed, leading the NFL in rushing yardage with 1,853 in 2002. In July 2004, just days before training camp was set to start, he called Coach Dave Wannstedt and retired. Williams went to India and Australia, studied yoga and holistic healing, and then made a one-year come-back. He fell afoul of the NFL drug testing program and was suspended for the 2006 season.

Earl Campbell and Ricky Williams's Heisman trophies sit in the lobby of the Moncrief-Neuhaus Athletic Complex, side by side on revolving pedestals in dark cherry cases. They are in symmetry, but they are no longer the focal point of the room. That addition was made in January, when a new case was put at the very front of the room. It now holds a crystal football, the one Vince Young kissed when the Longhorns won the national championship. And yet, as always at Texas, if there isn't now room for another Heisman, they'll make some.

In Vince We Trust

I n the end, it came down to faith for Vince Young. Just as his teammates and coaches had a belief in his unconquerable will, that all things were possible through Vince, Young had a belief that God held his destiny.

On Sunday morning, January 8, fresh off a redeye flight from Las Vegas, the Texas quarterback was sitting down with Reverend Samuel H. Smith Sr., the pastor of Mount Horeb Missionary Baptist Church in Houston's strife-ridden Fourth Ward.

Young was seeking counsel about his future. The Longhorn junior could return for his senior season, try to win another Big 12 and national championship, and improve on his Heisman Trophy runner-up finish to Reggie Bush of Southern California. Or he could turn professional, sign a multimillion-dollar contract, and take care of his mother, Felicia, and his uncle Keith Young, who had raised him as his own son.

It was the climax of a remarkable Texas career, which saw him go 30–2 as a starter, and lead Texas to victory nine times after trailing or being tied at halftime, including from second-half deficits of 21, 10, 10, 19, and, in the national championship game, 12 points.

"When you just look at numbers, and that doesn't tell the whole fact, but when the NCAA says 'only'—the only guy to throw for 3,000 and run for 1,000 in a season—that's pretty good, considering the history of college football," Texas offensive coordinator Greg Davis said of Young's legacy at Texas. "I think he'll go down certainly as one of the all-time great players if not the greatest. It's hard to pick out one guy. When I think back on those kind of questions, one thing that comes to my mind is the number of times he brought us back in the fourth quarter. With great quarterbacks that's what you talk about. He was certainly one of the most explosive athletes to play here."

At almost 6-5 and 225 pounds, Young had a much scrutinized and unorthodox throwing motion, but was third in the nation in pass efficiency rating as a junior. As a rusher, his three-year

Vince Young's moves weren't confined to running with the football. His relaxed, confident aura galvanized the Longhorns on their BCS title run.

total of 3,127 was fifth on the school's all-time list, behind Ricky Williams, Cedric Benson, Earl Campbell, and Chris Gilbert. In two Rose Bowls, in both of which he earned offensive player of the game honors, he rolled up 372 and 467 yards total offense, breaking the Rose Bowl career record set by Washington quarterback Mark Brunell in three appearances from 1991 to '93.

Young could beat some of the best defenders in the college game and make it look easy. "He has 'it,'" said teammate Michael Griffin. "The things he's done, even when you rewind it you think, how'd he do that? Not everybody can do that."

Young also had the ultimate confidence of his team, which he earned with his brash attitude and ability to back it up. Griffin said Young's performance against Michigan in a 38–37 victory in the 2005 Rose Bowl set the tone for their championship run.

After being benched against Missouri in 2004, Vince Young bounced back with a career-turning day at Texas Tech.

"Watch how he took over the game," Griffin said. "Michigan had a great corner on that team [Marlin Jackson] and he wasn't scared of him. They had a big safety [Ernest Shazor] and he wasn't scared of him. He just kept going after them. That whole week he's telling us this is our game, let's go win it. I've never heard him say anything like, 'This is a good team we're playing and I don't know.' All you every heard come out of Vince Young's mouth was win. Coach Brown even had to calm him down, tell him he can't underestimate anybody. He's just got that confidence we're going to win."

Now, with the ultimate team prize behind him, he asked Reverend Smith for his guidance. Smith told him he was leaning toward Young returning for his senior year, but had a dream the night before about a fleet of fishermen trying to catch one rainbow trout. Smith told him that trout shouldn't be caught—and that Young was that trout.

"I told him it was best to let him go free," Smith said. "He's got a lot to live in life, a lot to accomplish. I told him it was his time, his hour, to go forth and fulfill his future."

Seven hours later Young pulled up at the Moncrief-Neuhaus Athletic Complex in a white stretch limo, met with Mack Brown, and then, in a room packed with reporters, announced his decision to turn professional.

Three and a half months later, after speculation that Young could free-fall as far as the middle of the first round, the Tennessee Titans took him with the third pick of the NFL draft, tabbing him as their quarterback of the future. They, too, had faith.

11

A MAN NAMED MACK

When John Mackovic was reassigned after six occasionally glorious, often tumultuous seasons as Texas head coach, the Longhorns looked to men with proven records of working miracles.

First they looked north, to Gary Barnett at Northwestern. Barnett, a master motivator who led his Wildcats in singing "High Hopes" as they walked to practice on Fridays, had led long-time doormat Northwestern to back-to-back Big Ten titles and a Rose Bowl berth, an accomplishment once

Mack Brown's storybook first season at Texas included a victory in Lincoln that ended Nebraska's national-best home winning streak.

described as leading the Swiss Army to victory in World War II.

At the same time, they called East, to Mack Brown at North Carolina. Texas athletic director DeLoss Dodds had heard former OU AD Donnie Duncan, who had tried to hire Brown in the mid 1990s when he was at North Carolina, sing the praises of a man who took a 1–10 program at a basketball school and made it a top 5 team.

"I really didn't know between the two of them," Dodds said of his first inclination. "Some of our fans, and those who know the inside scoop, thought Barnett was the No. 1 choice."

Dodds met with Barnett in Chicago. Barnett had long coveted the Texas job, saying privately it was one of two jobs he wanted. On a recruiting trip, one of his assistants met with Wildcat alums in Austin and asked about the area, the best places to live, the best schools. He wanted the job and, working from a per-ceived position of strength, he acted like Texas wanted him and he knew it.

The Longhorns did, at first, but Barnett overplayed his hand, and his confidence was seen as arrogance. Texas had already been down that road. After meeting Barnett, Dodds and booster Tom Hicks flew to Atlanta to meet with Brown at the Four Seasons. They met him before breakfast, as a prelude to a roundtable with the selection committee, which included Darrell Royal.

"I knew he was the one after that conversation," Dodds said. "The way he is now—he was that way then."

Borrowing a page from Royal, who grilled Dana X. Bible on the committee members' names and backgrounds when he came in for the interview, Brown debriefed Dodds.

"He asked me who was in the room, where they were sitting," Dodds said. "Then he goes in there and blows that bunch out of the water. Never missed a name. He answered all their questions. It was a slam dunk."

For Texas, anyway. The plan was for the committee to meet Barnett in St. Louis that afternoon, but the meeting was scrapped. Barnett, arriving back in Chicago, told a staffer, "I think I done [screwed] this thing up." He then pulled out of the race.

Brown, however, wasn't fully sold. After the committee met privately, Dodds headed up to Brown's hotel room. Brown sat in a chair with his wife Sally on the

Mack (right) and older brother Watson would both follow their grandfather into coaching football.

floor next to him, arm in arm. The sticking point wasn't money, it wasn't what Texas could do for him—it was what he felt he had promised to do for North Carolina. They talked of Sally's successful real estate business and her Carolina roots.

"They were just totally emotional about their love for North Carolina, what Mack had built at North Carolina and Mack's desire to win a national championship," Dodds said. "That he felt he couldn't do at North Carolina."

At last the pieces were in place to do it at Texas. Saddled only three years earlier in the disintegrating Southwest Conference, a league that had been riddled by NCAA probation, a poor television contract, the loss of marquee name Arkansas, and a mass exodus of the state's top recruits to the Big Ten, Southeastern Conference, Big Eight, and even the Pac 10, the Longhorns were in no position for a football renaissance.

The need reached critical mass in early 1994, when the College Football Association, which represented the television negotiating interests of all the major colleges outside the Big Ten and Pac 10, announced an extension with ABC and ESPN. The SEC, feeling it could do better than the CFA deal, broke away and on February 11 signed a five-year, $85 million deal with CBS. Three days later, the Atlantic Coast Conference signed an $80 million deal with ESPN and ABC. One day later, CBS added the Big East for $75 million, including basketball.

It was time to act. On February 24, Texas and fellow SWC schools Texas A&M, Texas Tech, and Baylor announced they were merging with the Big Eight to form the Big 12. Within days the league signed a $100 million television contract with ABC and Liberty Sports. The new league meant more respect, more visibility, and—perhaps most important—widened revenue streams that have allowed the school to make or plan

Watson and Mack sit with their father, Melvin Sr., who raised his boys to play sports and be model citizens.

facility improvements of more than $200 million since the merger.

Dodds offered Brown the job and a quick plane trip to Austin. Brown told him he promised the UNC president and athletic director that he would talk to them first. And, he told Dodds, he needed to talk to his team. Then he told Dodds he'd call him in the morning.

"I sat in the office until four o'clock and he didn't call," Dodds recalled. "He called [Chuck] Neinas, former head of College Football Association, and Donnie Duncan, 'Hey, guys, you've got to help me.' I don't know if either made a call, but shortly after that I heard from Mack."

Texas had another jet waiting at the regional airport. Brown was on his way to Texas.

Brown was an accomplished football standout at Cookeville, Tennessee, High School.

What the Longhorns got in Brown was a man who was groomed to be a lawyer—"There are a lot of successful doctors and lawyers, but there are not a lot of Mickey Mantles," his maternal grandmother Mary Ellen Watson told him—but born to be a coach.

And a coach at Texas. Shortly after taking the job, Brown said he had thought of what his grandfather, Eddie "Jelly" Watson, who passed away a year and a half earlier at age 91, would have demanded. "My granddad would kill me if I didn't take the Texas job," Brown said. "I think he'd say that the only reason I shouldn't come is if it's too hard. If anything, that's the reason I did come. I like to fix. I like to build. This is a challenge."

When he was two, Mack rode on the team bus with his older brother Watson and his grandfather. Eddie Watson, who in 32 seasons at Cookeville High School won 10 conference titles and became the winningest coach in the history of Central Tennessee, had the toddlers wear T-shirts, one with an X and the other an O. Brown's father, Melvin Sr., who had passed away in March 1997 of a brain aneurysm, also was a high school coach and administrator who later owned the town's main sporting goods store.

"I don't think he could have considered anything else but coaching," Brown's mother, Katherine, said.

They got a man who loved college football traditions. As a child, he wore out an LP with the classic school fight songs until he knew every one by heart. As an adult his office at Texas would look like a museum of his coaching stops, including head coaching stints at Appalachian State and Tulane, with everything from a collection of bowl watches under glass to a Texas football helmet made of Legos. He still has the telegram that Paul "Bear" Bryant sent him offering a scholarship to Alabama.

At the time of Brown's hiring, Dick Coop, a sports psychologist who remains one of Brown's closest friends, said, "He's a modern coach with traditional emphasis. It sounds like an oxymoron, but it's a neat fit. He's warm on the out- side, tough on the inside, the opposite of most coaches. I think players who try to test him will find that out."

From their first meeting with Brown, the Longhorn players were sold. "He had a swagger to him," Hicks said. "We liked the way he talked. At first glance we were thinking, 'This could be cool.' The No. 1 goal, he said, was there was too much tradition here that wasn't being used. Off the bat he said he wanted to bring back the former players, get them involved."

Former players like Johnny Treadwell and Ted Koy, who liked to visit prac- tice, got personal invitations to return. "He told us, 'We want the lettermen around, because you're part of the tra- dition we want to relive,'" Koy said. "I remember asking him when I went out

to practice for the first time, 'Coach, where can I stand?' He said, 'Wherever you want to.'"

Longtime fan Louis Murillo, who had also been turned away by Mackovic, got a message on his answering machine be- fore spring practice inviting him to come out. Murillo, figuring someone was fooling with him, played the tape for an old friend and former neighbor. "That's Coach Brown," Darrell Royal told Murillo.

"When they made Coach Royal, they broke the mold," Murillo said. "Then somebody put it back together and made Coach Brown. He gets along with fans, he gets along with players, he gets along with everybody. If the devil jumped up, he'd get along well with him."

Murillo recalled Brown's first spring,

when he, Brown, Royal, Ben Crenshaw, and Willie Nelson gathered at Cisco's, a popular East Austin restaurant, following Royal's charity golf tournament. When it came time to take a photo, Murillo said that Brown should be on the end.

"In case he has a bad year, then we can cut him out," Murillo said. Brown started laughing. "He has a good sense of humor, what it takes to be a good coach," Murillo said. "You can't buy charisma. Nobody sells it. You have to be born with it. And he was born with it."

Fred Akers, who had the unenviable job of following Royal, said Brown has managed to smooth over all the rifts that normally exist when a coaching change occurs.

"I guarantee you, when Darrell got here as head coach we probably had some alumni back away because 'I'm a D. X. Bible man,'" Akers said. "When I got here, some backed away because 'I'm a Darrell Royal man.' We probably had some back away when I left saying, 'I'm a Fred Akers man.' None of that changed until Mack came and brought all the factions together. Now everybody's saying, 'I'm a Texas man.'"

Brown emphasized the family atmosphere with his players. Though he developed a reputation as a top-notch recruiter, he relied heavily on his players to see who would fit and who wouldn't.

"You have to visit other schools to see the difference," said safety Michael Griffin. "You go to other schools and they look at you as just another player trying to join their team. Here the players have already accepted you, like, 'We're going out or come out and hang out at my house.'"

The reason for the quick acceptance is simple. "It's trust in the coaching staff. They bring in good people. They check out their whole history. Before Mack Brown offers you [a scholarship] he talks to your parents, talks to your coaches, talks to your friends. Once you commit, he asks you about other guys we're recruiting. 'Do you know this guy? What do you know about him?'"

Almost unfailingly, Brown knows plenty himself. Tackle Justin Blalock remembers being impressed by Brown's preparation. "He'd remembered I'd come to a camp my eighth-grade year and put on the questionnaire I'd taken the SAT and scored well on it."

Said Griffin, "He knew Marcus was my twin brother. All the other coaches thought he was my younger brother. Knowing those kinds of details makes a difference."

Linebacker Anthony Hicks tore knee ligaments in 1998 on a crack-back block by Texas Tech receiver Derek Dorris. After the Longhorns beat Tech in Austin the next season, Hicks ran up to Dorris as the Tech receiver was headed to the sideline after the final gun. He grabbed Dorris's arm.

"Everything's okay," Hicks said.

"Thanks, man," Dorris said.

And they shook hands. It was a low-key moment, easily lost in the crowded on-field confusion after a game.

A few minutes later, as the players gathered around the middle of the locker room, Brown gave his postgame speech. At some point he called out Hicks and told the team what Hicks had done.

"You can't teach class like that," Brown said. "I don't know if anybody else saw it, but I did."

Hicks marvels at Brown's ability to be all-knowing. "It's amazing how he always knows what's going on with his team. It's like a shepherd, always in tune with his flock."

Though Brown stresses self-discipline and accountability, he allows his players input into decisions. "He let us wear black shoes and socks, let us play music during warm-ups at practice," Griffin said. "Anything he can do, whatever he is asked, if it's in his power he'll do it."

Brown's first priority in restoring the Longhorns was to get its patriarch, Royal, back involved.

Ted Koy, who played for Royal and has gotten to know Brown well, sees several uncanny similarities between the two men.

"One is their overall character," Koy said. "I've never seen Coach Royal holler and scream. I've never seen Mack Brown holler and scream. They don't need to.

Both have the mystique that commands respect. There is a difference, and it's a generational thing. We were scared to death of Coach Royal. That's just the way it was. I was watching practice one day and Limas Sweed came up to Mack and put his arm around him. Five minutes later, Mack was correcting him on something and it was all, 'Yes sir, no sir.'"

Royal became a fixture at practice, riding the sidelines in a golf cart, and Brown rarely let a media opportunity go by without invoking some lesson he had learned from Royal.

One of the first concerned the expectations at Texas. Brown said he asked Royal what were the pluses and minuses of coaching at Texas.

"Twenty million people care about Texas football," Royal said of the pluses.

And the minuses?

"Twenty million people care about Texas football," Royal repeated.

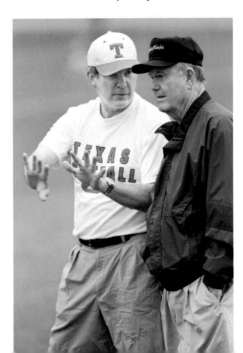

One of Brown's first tasks was to reunite a fractured Longhorn family, which he did first by embracing Darrell Royal.

Brown had a clue about the expectations and he had a better feel for the team that was coming back after a 4–7 mark in 1997. He had a new quarterback, a great running back, a solid offensive line, and a defense that needed a drastic infusion of talent. He also knew that the early schedule, featuring road games at UCLA and Kansas State, could be a backbreaker.

Anthony Hicks said the Longhorns had long focused on the game against the Bruins, hoping for redemption for the 66–3 embarrassment from 1997.

"Our mind-set going into that season was: UCLA," Hicks said. "Once again, another game that would set the tone for the season. We were angry at them for what they did to us and then we go out and lose. That was a devastating blow. Then the next week at Kansas State, emotionally and confidence-wise we weren't there."

With the season in the balance, Brown and his staff pushed the reset button. "The coaches talked to us and said it was a brand-new season," Hicks

said. "We went back to basics—and they worked the shit out of us."

Texas rebuilt its psyche with one-sided victories over Rice, Iowa State, and Oklahoma, the last a 34–3 victory that hastened the exit of Sooner Coach John Blake at season's end. On Halloween afternoon, the Longhorns went to Nebraska, where the Cornhuskers hadn't lost since dropping a 36–21 game to No. 4 Washington in 1991.

It was a different Texas team, with Major Applewhite established at quarterback, Ricky Williams on his way to the Heisman Trophy, and a defense prepared for the Cornhuskers' option-I attack. "By that game we had a unit, a togetherness," Hicks said. "Before we had everyone just trying to fill out their roles. Now we could play them. We went in with the mentality that we had nothing to lose, don't make this game bigger than it is."

The unranked Longhorns left with a 20–16 victory, but their hopes for a Big 12 South title collapsed in a 42–35 shootout in Lubbock, when the Long-

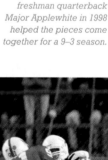

The emergence of redshirt freshman quarterback Major Applewhite in 1998 helped the pieces come together for a 9–3 season.

*Under Brown and coordinator Carl Reese
a defense that had been among the nation's
worst the year before contained
the Nebraska option attack in 1998.*

horns' lack of secondary depth was exposed. They would finish strongly, beating South Division champion Texas A&M 26–24 at home and then rolling No. 25 Mississippi State in the Cotton Bowl to finish Brown's first season with an impressive 9-3 and ranked No. 15.

Brown had set the bar. He had set it higher than anyone had expected after a 4–7 record in 1997, but all that meant was he had to keep bettering it.

The 1999 season started on a bad note, when the Longhorn special teams had three punts blocked in a 23–20 upset loss to North Carolina State in a game the Longhorns had added at the behest of the Black Coaches Association. Brown learned two valuable lessons—tighten the punt protection and don't schedule any more games than you have to.

The Longhorns beat Bob Stoops's first Oklahoma team, 38–28, having spotted the Sooners a 17-point lead. They handled No. 3 Nebraska at home 24–20, taking advantage of six Cornhusker turnovers, and had the Big 12 South wrapped up heading into their final regular-season game at Texas A&M.

Nine days before the game the Aggies' bonfire collapsed, killing 12 current and former students. Brown remembered hearing the news on the way to work, learning that the information hotlines were overwhelmed and many parents had to travel to College Station to find out if their children were all right.

"I put myself in their position, what it was like," Brown said. "For an hour and forty-five minutes, not knowing, that's helplessness."

A&M won 20–16, but the Longhorns already had a spot in their first Big 12 title game under Brown against North Division champion Nebraska. This time the Cornhuskers did not make mistakes, and their Black Shirt defense held Texas to a school record low -6 yards rushing. The slide continued in the Cotton Bowl, when an Arkansas team that understood the fundamental hatred their state has for Texas stunned an uninterested Longhorn team that was missing its top receiver, Kwame Cavil, and top defensive player, end Aaron Humphrey, who were among four players suspended thirty-six hours before kickoff for violating team rules.

While the Longhorns were in a three-game skid, the longest of any time during the Brown era, another question rose up. Applewhite, who was the Big 12 Offensive Player of the Year, tore his anterior cruciate ligament while scrambling late in the game and wouldn't be ready until fall practice. In his place sophomore Chris Simms had an impressive spring, and, with Longhorn coaches saying they were uncertain if Applewhite's knee was ready, Simms entered a quarterback rotation that would dog Brown for years to come.

So would another trend. Texas came into Dallas against an upstart Oklahoma team that had risen to No. 10 in the country, one spot ahead of the Longhorns, behind a junior-college quarterback named Josh Heupel and a revitalized defense. The Longhorns, featuring talented freshman receivers Roy Williams, B. J. Johnson, and Sloan Thomas, were dead set on jumping on the Sooners early and not spotting them a lead, as they had done the year before.

"I was stunned," cornerback Rod Babers said of the Sooners' early 17–0 lead in 1999. "I didn't know what was going on. I thought, 'Maybe these guys are that good . . .'"

Joked Brown the Monday before the 2000 rematch, "I was keeping track, trying to figure what four [quarters] times seventeen was."

He would quickly find out. The Sooners jumped to a 42–0 lead and rolled the stunned Longhorns 63–13, the worst defeat in the series since Oklahoma dominated 50–0 in 1908. Before the game, the Longhorns had taunted the Sooners, whom they'd beaten three straight times, by chanting "You're scared, you're scared."

After the game, Oklahoma linebacker Torrance Marshall ran up the tunnel yelling, "Who's scared now?"

Brown took full responsibility for the massacre. "You can't look anywhere else," he said. "Nobody can screw it up as badly as I did today."

Texas dropped all the way to No. 25, but worked its way back up to No. 12 before blowing a halftime lead against No. 8 Oregon and losing in the Holiday Bowl, 35–30.

The Longhorns returned a team talented enough to begin the 2001 season ranked No. 5, but they also still had a quarterback controversy that was about to explode. Simms, who came to Texas as the *Parade Magazine* offensive player

Texas was denied a spot in the BCS title game in 2001 when Colorado, aided by four Chris Simms turnovers, upset the Longhorns in the Big 12 championship game.

of the year, supplanted the lightly re-cruited Applewhite as starter. All seemed well until Simms threw four intercep-tions in a 14–3 loss to Oklahoma, and fans howled for Applewhite's return.

Simms, though, stuck at quarterback and won six games, including a 21–7 vic-tory at Texas A&M, where two years ear-lier he had lost his first college start. Texas appeared headed to the Holiday Bowl, but Oklahoma, which had earlier been upset by a precocious four-touchdown performance by Texas A&M freshman quarterback Reggie McNeal, faltered in its Bedlam Series showdown against rival Oklahoma State, 16–3. Texas, suddenly, had backed into the Big 12 championship game against Col-orado, a team it had beaten 41–7 in Austin.

Two weeks earlier it appeared a mor-tal lock that Nebraska and Oklahoma would meet for the Big 12 title. Then Colorado stunned Nebraska 62–36 and OSU upset the Sooners in Norman, knocking the Sooners out of the na-tional championship race. Hours before the Longhorns took the field against the Buffalos at Texas Stadium, Tennessee upset Florida 34–32, which gave the Longhorns this path: beat Colorado and they were in the Rose Bowl playing for the national title.

Simms, however, turned the ball over four times in the first half as Colorado took a 29–17 halftime lead. Applewhite replaced Simms after the last turnover, but could only rally the Longhorns to a 39–37 margin.

After the last turnover, Simms was booed by the predominantly Texas crowd. "It's something you'll always re-

In 2004, Derrick Johnson became the Longhorns' first Butkus Award winner as the nation's best linebacker.

*Cory Redding's goal-line leap sparked
the Longhorns to an emotional victory
over Mack Brown's former school,
North Carolina, in 2001.*

*Wide receiver Roy Williams was among
the most talented Longhorns of the early 2000s
whose football resume did not include
a victory over Oklahoma.*

member," Simms said. "It's one of those things that makes you wonder who's behind you, who's not."

Said Applewhite, "Chris has taken a beating he does not deserve."

Brown, however, was quick to name Applewhite as the starter in the senior's last game, another Holiday Bowl appearance, this one against Washington State. Applewhite passed for a school single-game best 473 yards as the Longhorns won 47–43.

"When you sit back and look at things, the first thing that comes to mind is as they are unfolding you take as much information as you can gather about a situation and you make your play, whether it's in playing cards or game-planning," said offensive coordinator Greg Davis. "We certainly won a bunch of ballgames through that era but we didn't win a championship in that era. Our job as coaches is to try and win every game. Based on the last game we had played, the Big 12 championship, Major deserved to start. Everything in that whole era can be summed up just like that decision was made."

Now that era was over. In 2002, Simms was the clear-cut starter. What he didn't have was a victory over Oklahoma, and that wasn't lost on him.

"It's a great week to be me," Simms told reporters the Monday before the game, anticipating redemption.

Texas took a 17–14 lead into the fourth quarter, but the Longhorn de-

fense suddenly couldn't stop Quentin Griffin, who gained 102 of his 248 yards in the final period as the Sooners scored three touchdowns and rallied for a 35–24 victory.

Again the Longhorns battled back after the loss, winning 17–14 at No. 17 Kansas State when sophomore Dusty Mangum kicked a 27-yard field goal with 1:32 left and Marcus Tubbs blocked Jared Brite's potentially game-tying 36-yard field goal in the final seconds. Again, the Longhorns wasted opportunity. Texas Tech beat the No. 4 Longhorns 42–38 in Lubbock, a game that would come back to haunt the Longhorns when they dropped to No. 10 and out of the BCS mix.

In 2003 the Longhorns made a significant change. Mac McWhorter, who had joined the staff and shared offensive line duties with Tim Nunez the previous season, took over when Nunez was reassigned. McWhorter's first act was to give the unit an identity.

"Other than soft," said guard Mike Garcia.

Indeed, the Longhorns' inability to grind it out against Oklahoma had labeled the unit. McWhorter had the linemen select a more favorable moniker. They settled on Trench Hogs. McWhorter, a stickler for detail, treated them as such.

"If the schedule said we were going to spend a minute on a run drill, we spent a minute on a run drill," Garcia said.

"Not a second more, not a second less. And in that minute we'd get six to eight reps."

McWhorter said repetitions were the secret to line cohesiveness. "Blocking plays are almost like snowflakes," he said. "Every time you mesh on a block, or work to another level to get the linebacker, there's a little degree of difference."

There was a bigger reason the Longhorn line became dominant, but that wouldn't happen until 2004: Vince Young became Vince Young. The week after he got benched for a lackluster performance against Missouri, Young was given a tape of his highlights, complete with the sounds of television announcers oohing and ahhing. The idea was to remind Young how good he could be if he just relaxed.

"There were so many so critical of him that we took films of his being suc-cessful and said, 'This is who you are. This is what you can do,'" Brown said.

In a 51–21 victory at Texas Tech, Young ran the ball on eight of 11 plays on the Longhorns' first scoring drive and completed passes on two others. He ran or threw for five touchdowns, and although his passing still wasn't top-notch—he threw two interceptions early in each of the next three games—he was finding his rhythm.

So was the Longhorn defense, which made a believer out of Tech Coach Mike Leach, who was used to his quarterbacks shredding the Longhorns' man-to-man schemes.

"Occasionally you read this business that the University of Texas is soft," Leach said. "Well, we're a helluva lot softer."

After getting ripped apart by Washington State in the 2003 Holiday Bowl, defensive coordinator Carl Reese resigned to fish full-time in Missouri. Brown hired former Kansas City Chiefs defensive coordinator Greg Robinson, a move first greeted with skepticism because Robinson had been let go only a week earlier because of the Chiefs' play-off collapse against Indianapolis.

Robinson built the defense around linebacker Derrick Johnson, used a better mixture of man and zone coverage, and improved the secondary. That improvement only seemed to mock the Longhorns when they held Oklahoma to 12 points but their own offense was shut out.

Brown's winning percentage of 81.4 in his first eight seasons ranks second to Dave Allerdice's 82.5 among coaches who spent more than three years at Texas.

Critics wondered aloud if Brown would ever beat the Sooners, or should even get the chance. No Texas coach who had lost five straight to the Sooners ever beat them again. The Longhorns, despite outstanding talent like receiver Roy Williams, halfback Cedric Benson, and linebacker Derrick Johnson, appeared fated to be great at a time when the Sooners were greater.

Brown's losses to Oklahoma aggravated fans, but he had revitalized a program that sorely needed it. Television revenue nearly doubled to $4.1 million a year since Brown took over and there's a fifty-person-deep waiting list for the sixty-four luxury suites at Royal-Texas Memorial Stadium. Season ticket sales rose from 39,700 in 1997 to 66,301, where they were capped until the current round of renovations are finished and capacity tops 90,000.

"Would I trade my football program for Oklahoma's?" said San Antonio businessman Red McCombs, for whom the Texas business school is named. "I wouldn't trade it if they gave me the football program and the whole state."

Brown's reputation for getting the Longhorns to the door but not being able to, as Houston Oilers Coach Bum Phillips once said of his team's string of near misses, "kick the damn thing in," allowed him to build a friendship with golfer Phil Mickelson, whom he met at a 2003 tournament in Dallas.

They made a pact. They would both

remake their images. They would both win the big one. When Mickelson won the 2004 Masters, he sent Brown one of the pin flags and a message. "I got mine," Mickelson told Brown. "Now it's your turn."

In early 2005, Brown completed the puzzle. He wooed Gene Chizik, who had coordinated unbeaten Auburn's defense in 2004, to replace Robinson, who had gotten the head coaching job at Syracuse. He had a redoubtable quarterback in Young, a deep backfield, the most physical and talented offensive line in decades, and the best defensive talent since the glory days of the early 1980s.

Eight years after Brown arrived, after a litany of close calls and heartbreaking losses, all the pieces were in place, all the hurdles cleared. They had beaten the Sooners, won Brown's first conference title in record fashion, and made it to the BCS title game. In a moment of reflection, Brown recalled what Tom Hicks had asked him when they met for the first time in Atlanta. "Tom's

*One side chants "Texas,"
the other "Fight." It's one
of the most distinctive
cheers in all of college
football.*

first question to me was, 'Can we bring a national championship to Texas?'" Brown recalled. I'll never forget it be-cause my answer was 'I can't, but we can.'"

They would now get their chance.

Brown and Cedric Benson run off the field after the Longhorns came back from a 28-point deficit against Oklahoma State in 2004, a victory he credited with starting the run toward the national championship.

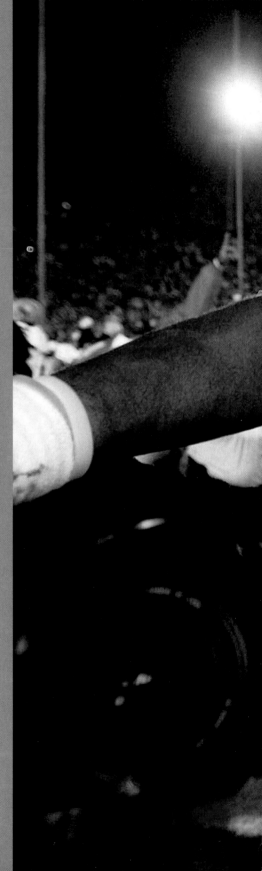

12

TAKE DEAD AIM

The word the Longhorns had long awaited came on Sunday afternoon, December 4, 2005, when the Bowl Championship Series pairings were announced. They would be in the Rose Bowl against Southern Cal, the team they'd been gearing for since midseason.

Shortly after the announcement some players

Motivated by his Heisman snub,
Vince Young flashes the pose after beating Southern Cal
and the previous two winners of the trophy,
Matt Leinart and Reggie Bush.

gathered in the rose-strewn players' lounge at the Moncrief-Neuhaus Athletic Complex to meet the media and answer questions about their emotions, their expectations, and their feelings about playing the Trojans.

Longhorn defensive tackle Rod Wright said dominating the Trojans, not just winning the game, was their goal.

"If you prepare like that, then it can happen," Wright said. "We're not going to be overwhelmed."

"Why should they intimidate us? We're the same team," Vince Young said the next day. "We've been to the granddaddy of them all. We've played in the big games. We've got a nineteen-game winning streak. All that scary stuff—we're not going to be scared."

Overall they were confident and fairly complimentary—just not complimentary enough to suit their head coach.

Mack Brown wasn't there but he was worried about some of the quotes coming out of his camp. Brown had been in New York City attending the National Football Foundation Awards dinner, an annual event that honors college football's best, but word got back to him that some of players weren't as lavish with praise about the Trojans as he would have hoped. Years of coaching had taught him you don't make the block bully mad. Or underestimate him.

"A couple of kids on Sunday when we accepted the bid said something like 'USC's not very good,'" Brown said. "I

told them, 'Anybody who said they aren't any good is foolish. Don't look like a fool.'"

Before Brown could figure out a way to regain their attention without working them hard in practice, he got some unexpected help.

In recurring segments hyping the Rose Bowl, ESPN began pitting the Trojans against the greatest college teams of all time in a mock playoff to determine not the '05 champion, but the greatest team of all time. The network pitted USC vs. 1988 Notre Dame. USC vs. 1995 Nebraska. And so on. It was a theme that would continue throughout December, as other media outlets joined the chorus.

"Every channel you turned on, somehow, some way, they were talking about it," Longhorn safety Michael Griffin said. "You could be watching some talk show and they'd talk about USC over Texas. Every day we had to hear was USC, USC, USC. We got to the game and said we have to put a stop to this. We wanted to make all of L.A. upset."

All of this was a fastball in Brown's wheelhouse.

"So the more ESPN talked about 'SC would have beaten the '88 Notre Dame team and 'SC would have beaten Nebraska our guys started to enjoy it, because it was good for us," Brown said. "Instead of crying like angry children, we said this is good. Let them keep bragging. We'll keep working."

"It was perfect for us," he added,

"after our players bought into it being perfect for us."

During the summer, at the suggestion of Sally Brown, the Longhorns had adopted a favorite saying of legendary Austin golf instructor Harvey Penick, who had tutored Ben Crenshaw and Tom Kite, among others. Penick's last instruction to any golfer heading to the course was simple. "Take dead aim," he would say.

Penick had passed away ten years earlier, only days before the Masters golf tournament. Crenshaw, who missed practice rounds to attend his mentor's funeral, went on to post one of the most stirring victories ever at Augusta, breaking down after he sank the winning putt on the eighteenth hole. Brown related the whole story to his team and had burnt-orange rubber bracelets made with the slogan inscribed. When word got out, the public clamored to buy the bracelets, but Brown insisted they would only be distributed to the players and coaches.

"Our theme means you can be bold and aggressive about anything you want as long as you're willing to do whatever it takes to reach your goals," Brown said when the slogan was announced in August.

The Longhorns had taken dead aim, on the Trojans and hype. To further accentuate their abilities to surprise as an underdog, Brown added two more motivational ploys. He told them of Presi-

dent Teddy Roosevelt's favorite motto, "Walk softly and carry a big stick," and emphasized that the Longhorns do their talking with their play, not their mouths. And he told them the story of the aptly named Trojan Horse.

It was around 1200 B.C. and Greeks were locked in an almost decade-long war with Troy. Though they were able to defeat the Trojans in many battles, they were unable to penetrate the walls of the city of Troy. Odysseus, leader of the Greek army, devised a way to take advantage of the Trojans' overconfidence.

Odysseus had a giant wooden horse built and loaded it with troops. The rest of the Greek fleet sailed away, as if conceding defeat. The Trojans, celebrating an apparent victory, brought the horse into the gates. In the dead of night, while most of Troy was sleeping or too drunk from celebration, the Greeks climbed out of the horse and took the city.

"So we're gonna keep our mouths shut, we're going to slip in in the horse, the Trojans are going to go to sleep, and we're going to attack," Brown told his team.

Stripped of its hype, the game was still everything any college football fan could want. It would be Texas, winner of 19 straight, against Southern Cal, winner of 34 straight, for the national title. Vince Young vs. Matt Leinart. Reggie Bush vs. Texas's defensive speed. Bevo vs. Traveler. One school with great tradition

Young and tight end David Thomas were a combination the Trojans couldn't stop.

against another. "It's a magical matchup this year," Rose Bowl chief executive Mitch Dorger said when the selections were announced. "We have the last two Rose Bowl game winners. . . . We have the last two Rose Bowl MVPs. . . . We will have at least three Heisman finalists and possibly two Heisman Trophy winners in the game."

One more piece of motivation remained. The 2005 Heisman winner wouldn't be announced until December 10. Young joined USC's Reggie Bush and Matt Leinart for the award presentation at the Nokia Theater on Times Square in New York City. Most reliable polls of Heisman voters had Bush comfortably ahead with Young second, but the headstrong Texas quarterback wasn't buying.

When they announced Bush's name as the winner, Young was stunned. He had received only 79 first-place votes to Bush's 784 and received more second-place votes than anybody else in the award's history, but he seemed more annoyed than disappointed.

"I'm just disappointed for my fans, especially for my teammates and my family for not representing them in the right way," Young told the media after the presentation. "I feel like I let my guys down, let my family down, let the whole cities of Austin and Houston down."

Wrote *Austin American-Statesman* columnist Kirk Bohls, who'd covered the Longhorns since he was a student at Texas in the early 1970s, "Beware, Southern Cal. Beware of the slighted

Cedric Griffin's first-quarter hit on USC fullback Brandon Kirtman announced that the Longhorns weren't going to concede anything to the team some had anointed as the best in college football history.

one, the one with the scowl, the unforgiving. Be on the lookout in just more than three weeks for a man possessed. That would be Vince Young. Just between us, I'm wondering if he will smile again between now and Jan. 4. Vince is angry. And that's a good thing for Texas."

Now all Texas had to do was play the game.

It didn't start well for the Longhorns. After the defense forced a three-and-out, punt returner Aaron Ross lost the ball while fighting for extra yards. USC recovered and five plays later went up 7–0.

When the Longhorns got the ball back, they drove to the USC 48, where they faced a fourth-and-one.

"That was a message to our team that we had to score a lot of points and that we were coming to win. We told our team we would go for it when we crossed the 50," Brown said. "We didn't come to lay up. Take dead aim. That was the message."

Running back Selvin Young probed the left tackle but was driven back for a loss of 1.

USC drove to the Longhorn 17, but on fourth-and-one Texas stopped Leinart on a quarterback sneak. Momentum had swung, but USC grabbed it right back when on the second play of the second quarter Leinart threw a screen pass to Bush, who broke up the middle. As Aaron Ross tackled him, Bush inexplicably tried to flip the ball to

his right to receiver Brad Walker, who was trailing the play. The ball came loose and Frank Okam recovered for the Longhorns.

Texas got a 42-yard David Pino field goal to get on the scoreboard with 10:38 left in the first half, but USC didn't let up. Leinart looked off the safeties and then lofted a ball deep to Steve Smith. Longhorn strong safety Michael Griffin raced over and made a leaping catch at the Longhorn 1. Officials ruled it an incompletion.

"I didn't think my foot got in," Griffin conceded. "I knew I caught the ball. I started protesting to buy some time. I knew if they played the next play they couldn't go back and review it. Aaron Harris ran up and said, 'You're in, you're in.' Cedric Griffin did too. Then I saw the replay and I knew."

The play was reviewed and overturned. Then Texas benefited from a call that could have been reviewed but wasn't when Young capped the following drive by pitching to Selvin Young, though his knee was clearly down at the 12, for a touchdown.

Ramonce Taylor scored on a 30-yard sweep to the right and Mario Danielo added a 43-yard field goal with two seconds left in the half. Texas went into the locker room leading 16–10.

Texas had found its rhythm, and its attack. During the game the Longhorns would use only two formations, employing one of them—a one-back, three-

facing page: USC was effective running the ball between the tackles with halfback LenDale White, who scored three touchdowns.

Ramonce Taylor's 30-yard touchdown run helped stake Texas to a 16–3 lead in a first half that was controlled by the defenses.

receiver set—almost exclusively. Young was finding his matchups, particularly David Thomas, who would close his Longhorn career with a school tight end record 10 catches, for 88 yards.

Brown gathered his team. "How much fun is this?" he said, breaking into a huge grin. "All the talk's gone, all the stuff's gone. We have thirty minutes."

The second half turned into a tag-team exchange of scoring. USC regained the lead 17–16 early in the third quarter. Texas went up 23–17 on the next drive. USC moved ahead 24–23.

That's the way the fourth quarter started, and it appeared the Trojans would do as they had done for 34 games, and that was finish strongly. Bush, who had trouble breaking containment for most of the game, outran the Longhorns down the right sideline for a 26-yard score. After a 34-yard Pino field goal, Leinart drove the Trojans 80 yards in five plays, hitting Dwayne Jarrett on a post play that not only gave the Trojans a

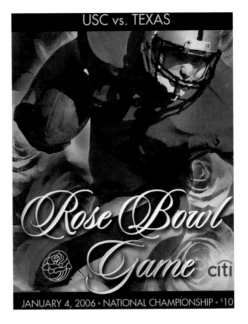

USC vs. TEXAS

Rose Bowl Game citi

JANUARY 4, 2006 • NATIONAL CHAMPIONSHIP • $10

233

TAKE DEAD AIM

38–26 lead, but knocked Longhorn cornerback Tarell Brown out with a broken forearm and gave safety Griffin a neck sprain.

Relying almost entirely on his passing, Young drove the Longhorns from their own 31 to the USC 17, where on first-and-ten, he took the snap, reversed field, and broke to his right, cutting up

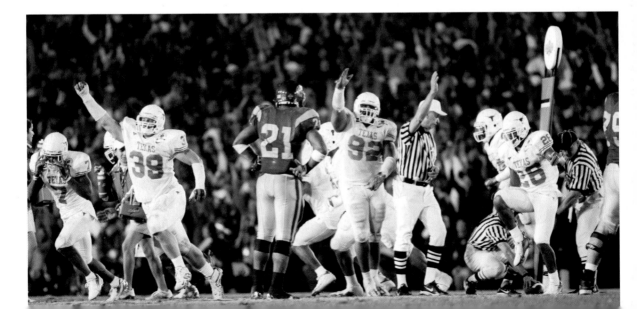

between a diving Trojan defender for a touchdown that cut the USC lead to 38–33.

USC had been successful running LenDale White the entire game, and tried to bludgeon the Longhorn front seven and the clock with the 235-pound junior. White gained 5 yards on a third-and-seven at midfield, setting up a decision on fourth-and-two at the Texas 45.

USC Coach Pete Carroll, seeing what Young could do if given another chance, wanted to end it right there.

Like his counterpart, Brown made an all-or-nothing gamble. "We basically said passes don't count," Brown said. "We had to make a calculated guess that's what they're going to do. So [safety] Michael Huff's in the backfield. If they had faked it and completed the pass it would have been a touchdown. And we told our players, 'Don't worry about the pass. If they throw it and

catch it run down there and hug them and congratulate them on winning the national championship.'"

USC went instead with what worked all night, sending White into the line with a lead blocker. Texas end Brian Robison submarined and got a hand on White's ankle and the middle of the Longhorn defense stopped White a yard short.

"Once we made that stop it was automatic," Blalock said. "We were going to win that game."

As Young headed onto the field, linebacker Aaron Harris and cornerback Cedric Griffin got in his face and screamed, "What you gonna do?"

"That kind of pumped me up. I went up to my offensive line, my teammates, got in the huddle, told a little joke and everybody laughed and stayed relaxed and we took over."

USC, in a state of defensive desperation it hadn't experienced all season, began blitzing cornerbacks, linebackers, and safeties, all trying to pressure Young into a game-ending mistake.

"They were throwing everything in the book at us, trying to confuse us," Blalock said. "They were dropping defensive linemen into coverage and using faster guys to contain. Whatever they could do to try to create havoc."

Starting at its own 44 with 2:09 and two timeouts left, Texas moved the ball downfield. Anticipating an all-out blitz, Young threw a screen to Taylor on first

Eight yards, 26 seconds, and 35 years of history were what stood between the Longhorns and a national championship.

down for a loss of 2. He threw an incompletion to Limas Sweed and then on third and 12, he hit Quan Cosby on the right sideline for seven yards. USC, though, was penalized for a face mask and the Longhorns had a first down at the Trojans' 46.

Young sandwiched completions of 9 and 17 yards to Brian Carter around a 7-yard gain to give Texas a first and 10 at the 13. Young tried to hit Sweed in the back of the end zone but threw long. After a Texas timeout with 30 seconds left, Young gained 5 on a keeper and then went back to Sweed on a quick slant, but the ball was just beyond his fingers.

It was fourth-and-five from the USC 8: Twelve seconds remained. Twelve seconds and 35 years.

Before the Longhorns left for Los Angeles, Greg Davis asked Young what play he'd run if there was one shot from the 8 to win the game. Young said, "You'd probably want Menu 2, but I'd want a quarterback draw."

Menu 2, off the list of plays in the Longhorns' no-huddle offense, had Young line up in the shotgun with four receivers split wide and the halfback set to Young's right. The receivers on the left crisscrossed; the two on the right did hook patterns. The halfback drifted into the flat.

Said Davis to Young, "Menu 2 gives you the quarterback draw."

Back in Dallas, former Longhorns Anthony Hicks and Ricky Brown, watching on television and unable to sit, looked at each other. "This is the play," they said. "This is where legends are made."

Young took the snap. USC end Lawrence Jackson took a deep rush and left tackle Jonathan Scott pushed him past Young and to the ground. Left guard Kasey Studdard picked up blitzing linebacker Collin Ashton. On the right side of the Longhorn line the Trojans were in a zone blitz, with end Frostee Rucker dropping back and defensive back Josh Pinkard blitzing between the guard and tackle.

Sensing Jackson coming behind him from his left, Young headed to his right off tackle Justin Blalock's leveling of Pinkard and put a move on Rucker, who gave brief chase and then dove short of Young's feet.

It was now a mere footrace to history.

"I knocked the safety down and the next thing I know I see No. 10 headed for the corner," said Blalock, who immediately raised his hands to signal touchdown. "There it is. There's no way he'll be stopped."

From the far end zone at the Rose Bowl, former linebacker Pat Culpepper watched through his binoculars. "I was the one who yelled, with a thousand others, 'He's got it,' before the hole opened up."

Sitting nearby, halfback Ted Koy watched intently. "Even when you go

back to when I played, every team that wins the national championship, there are always a few other teams that except for a few ifs, a few plays, could be there. You have to be lucky. Finally Texas had it."

Young slid into the right corner of the end zone, and after his run for the two-point conversion on a quarterback draw the Longhorns were 19 seconds away from the national title leading 41–38.

UT squibbed the kickoff and USC took over at its own 31. Leinart immediately hit Bush with a shovel pass that gained 27 yards to the Texas 42. One more short, quick gain and the Trojans were in position for a game-tying field goal. Leinart dropped back, was flushed to his left, and patiently looked for his receiver before aiming for Jarrett on the sideline. The ball was high, the clock

had run out, and the title belonged to Texas.

Players and coaches streamed onto the field. Confetti rained down. Old Smokey, the Longhorns' cannon, boomed. Back in Austin, houses shook with the screaming of fans; car horns sounded and backyard fireworks pierced the sky.

Fred Akers, watching with his wife, Diane, from the living room of his daughter Staci's house in Austin, where they were babysitting his grandchildren, felt the wave. "It made me feel much better. I was so proud about what Mack and his staff have done. Texas deserves that. Their expectations need to be realized. It's surprising it took that many years. It also tells you how hard it is to get it done."

In his living room in Atlanta, former

Brown savors the victory with his mother, Katherine, in the chaotic postgame locker room area.

Longhorn receiver Tony Jones rejoiced. "I was up," he said, "dancing along with Vince."

In Dallas, Anthony Hicks and Ricky Brown looked at each other in disbelief. "We were like, 'They did it! Did this really just happen?'" Hicks said. "Did they really just win the national championship?"

In the locker room after the game, Brown told his team he wasn't going to cry, because he expected them to win. He reminded them of Matthew McConaughey's talk of reaching their goal and then living their dream. Brown also offered them some sage perspective for the long term.

"When you are fifty-four, I don't want this to be the best thing you ever did in your life," he said, adding, "If you have enough to be a national champion, you'll have enough to be a great citizen and role model, a great father and leader of your family. That's what we expect of you when you leave."

Outside the locker room Brown met up with his mother, Katherine. It was her seventy-seventh birthday. They exchanged congratulations and hugs.

"That was a very nice present," she told him.

Then even she couldn't resist.

"What are you going to get me next year?"

Eight years earlier, the memories of Jelly Watson and Melvin Brown and their love of college football had con-vinced Mack Brown to leave his beloved North Carolina for the challenges, and possibilities, of Texas. Now, in a private moment, Brown spoke to his father and grandfather.

"I don't want to sound religious or hokey about it, but I talked to them about it, knowing how proud they were," Brown said. "Part of the salute to the high school coaches I made after the game was to my dad and granddad, 'cause that's who they were, educators and coaches. I knew they were very proud, so I felt like they were standing there with me, in a strange way."

Back in Texas, the Trinity River, which snakes through the Dallas–Fort Worth area, began turning burnt orange near Grand Prairie. It started about 4 P.M. on January 3 as a pinkish-red hue, but by the time the Longhorns were celebrating the title it was burnt orange.

In Westlake, near Austin, fans left no doubt that the wait for the national championship was well worth it.

Longhorn fans saw it as a divine signal. Environmentalists attributed it to a spill of leftover dye used to create Longhorn national championship apparel.

University rules dictate that in the event of a national championship, the Texas Tower, the most recognizable building on campus, shall be bathed in orange light with certain windows lit to form a "1" figure on each side. The lights are supposed to burn that way for one night. This time it went on for two weeks, as people swarmed the campus to shoot photos, or just bask in the glow.

On January 15, the school held a celebration rally. An estimated 50,000 people came to Texas Royal-Memorial Stadium to see the team together one last time.

Texas Governor Rick Perry, a former Aggie yell leader, held up a pair of boots he won in a bet with California Governor Arnold Schwarzenegger. He looked at the team and said, "You made one Aggie proud. Hook 'em Horns."

U.S. Senator Kay Bailey Hutchinson won a bottle of California wine and a bouquet of yellow roses in a bet with California Senator Dianne Feinstein. Hutchison, who was a Longhorn cheerleader when they won their first national title in 1963, said it wasn't a high-risk bet. "All I did was believe in my Longhorns."

Said Brown in wrapping up the festivities, "This is the night we can say 'Hook 'em' and take down the little finger, because we are No. 1."

Governor Rick Perry, a former Texas A&M cheerleader, shows off the pair of boots he won in a wager with California Governor Arnold Schwarzenegger.

Brown said the best thing about winning the title is seeing the effect it's had on people, particularly Texas fans.

"They're just beside themselves," Brown said. "And the stories are wonderful. People tell me, 'I was with my dad at the '69 Cotton Bowl and had my son with me at the Rose Bowl and it was just a wonderful experience.' I hear those stories time and time again. But also I hear from the fans from Tech and A&M. All the fans in the state have been great. I've been really amazed by the reaction."

Brown tells the story of an exuberant Texas fan who buttonholed him one day after the Rose Bowl.

"You'll get a free pass the rest of your life," the man said, in full backslapping mode.

After the man walked away, a voice whispered in Brown's ear.

"That means you have six weeks," said Darrell Royal, "until spring practice starts."

The honeymoon, though, was far from over.

In early February 2006 the University of Texas Board of Regents unanimously approved a $390,000 pay raise that hiked his annual salary to $2.55 million, making him among the nation's highest-paid college football coaches. The board also approved a $150 million expansion and improvement project at Texas Royal-Memorial Stadium, including a new press box and an overhaul of the

*The 2005 Longhorns make a final grand entrance
at Royal-Texas Memorial Stadium for a rally
to celebrate the championship.*

north end zone that will move the stands closer to the field, add new office space, and push the stadium capacity from 80,082 to more than 90,000. The expansion was scheduled to be completed in 2008.

A few days later the Longhorns flew to Washington, D.C., to visit the White House to meet President Bush, who as governor of Texas got to know the coaches and staff during his frequent workouts in the Longhorns' weight room.

The players and staff gathered in the Rose Garden and Bush cracked that Brown's reputation as Mr. February no longer meant he was known more for his recruiting prowess than his football accomplishment. "Today, Mack, you're giving February—the title 'Mr. February'—a whole new meaning. This February you brought the national champs to the White House."

Bush continued, "But the thing that impressed me about the team and—you know, we can follow you here in Washington, D.C., just as well as we can follow you in Crawford—is that this team never figured out the word 'lose.' It never entered their vocabulary. Every time they walked on the field, you knew they were going to win. And perhaps one of the reasons why is because they were winners off the field as well."

As winners, they would reap the benefits. Brown, wary of the increasing demands on his time, spoke with several successful coaches about how to manage the national title aftermath. They all told him time management is a key.

"So if doesn't help us recruit, I'm not going to do it," Brown said, knowing visibility equals recruiting reach.

Around Austin, film director Peter Berg was making a pilot for *Friday Night Lights,* a television series based on the bestselling book of the same name by H. G. "Buzz" Bissinger, in Austin. (The book was also made into a feature film in 2004.) Through Brown's daughter Katherine, who's working in the movie business, Berg got word to Brown that he wanted him for a bit part.

Brown decided to do it as a favor to his daughter, but when he got on the set and was told he would play a booster for the Dillard Panthers, he warmed to the role. In the course of filming he got to spout lines like "Hope you understand the pressure of winning the championship here," and, in a spoof at himself, he said, "You don't have to have a great quarterback to win a championship. It's all coaching."

Joked Brown, "The fun part was when Peter Berg asked me if I needed a script and I said, 'No, I've had thirty-three years of parent and booster involvement, so I think I know what to say.'"

In early April, Texas Rangers owner and Longhorn booster Tom Hicks invited Brown and Royal to throw out the first pitch at the team's season opener

against the Boston Red Sox. Brown threw a low but passable strike. A week later he was at his first NASCAR race—quite a surprise because he spent ten years coaching in North Carolina, a car racing hotbed—waving the green flag to start the Samsung/Radio Shack 500 at Texas Motor Speedway.

Brown's spring itinerary also included speaking in Hickory, North Carolina, as a guest of Hickory native and Longhorn basketball coach Rick Barnes and delivering the commencement addresses for the University of Texas College of Liberal Arts and his high school in Cookeville, Tennessee.

"The good thing is we've been able to enjoy the moment," Brown said. "We've embraced winning the national championship and continued to work in a positive way for next year and not let complacency step in. The coaches are re-cruiting and the players are working harder than ever. We're able to ride the momentum of it instead of acting arrogant like it was something we deserved. People asked me if it was vindication. I'm not a vindictive person, so it didn't mean that to me."

If anyone could be forgiven for dishing out a few told-you-so's, it would have been Brown. "He's too smart for that," Royal said. "Actions speak louder than words sometimes."

Instead Brown insisted the title belonged to all Texas fans and every player who has ever worn the burnt orange. Ted Koy, halfback on the Longhorns' 1969 team, remembered the day after the January 2006 Rose Bowl, when he and his family went to lunch at In-N-Out Burger in Los Angeles. A USC fan in full regalia, stung by the loss and looking for a way to ease his pain, smugly asked

Koy when the Longhorns had last won a national title. Koy just smiled.

"It's great," he said. "Now I don't have to say thirty-five years. I can say last year. I don't have to drift off to ancient history. It's alive and well."

Anthony Hicks, who was there at the beginning of Brown's tenure and saw the makings of a future national title run, stood in awe alongside teammate Ricky Brown watching the celebration on television and was struck with a deep feeling of satisfaction.

"We don't know if they realize what they just did, for guys like me and Ricky, for their great stars, for guys like Lam Jones and Eric Metcalf, for the teams that knocked on the door and the teams that came within a play or two of knocking on the door," Hicks said later.

They understand what Mack Brown meant in an evening dinner address after the 2006 Mike Campbell Golf Tournament. Held at the Golf Club at Circle C near Austin, it's an opportunity for football alums from all across the country to come chase little dimpled white balls and tell huge white lies.

Brown stood up and asked the former players, "How do you like being national champions?"

Some looked at him quizzically. "It belongs to all of us," Brown said.

And so it does.

There was still some unfinished business. Sometime in early January 2006, when memories of the Rose Bowl were still fresh and plans were forming to renovate the facilities' lobby so it could accommodate all the new trophies, workmen affixed four more six-inch plastic letters following that lonely comma on the east wall of the Moncrief-Neuhaus Athletics Complex auditorium.

Up went "2005." They stopped there. Missing was a comma.

In late April, after spring practice wrapped, Mack Brown happened to take a look at the wall. He went to the man in charge of maintaining the building and told him what needed to be there. The comma went up.

"Because we always want to keep a comma up," Brown said. "And long after we're gone, hopefully, there'll be a comma up, for the next day, the next year. Forever."

*The flags spell it out for any fans who can't recognize
the only NCAA Division I-A school that's nicknamed
Longhorns and wears burnt orange.*

The Longhorns enter Royal-Texas Memorial Stadium after touching a plaque at the base of the scoreboard dedicated to defensive back Freddie Steinmark, who died of cancer in 1971.

George Schroeder, whose tremendous book *Hogs!* blazed the trail for this work, gave my name to Bob Mecoy, who got the project off the ground. Thanks to both of you for providing this opportunity.

Brett Valley, my editor, helped shepherd an author who had never produced a book on his own through the demanding process, which included tight deadlines and unexpected turns in the road. Copyeditor Tom Pitoniak deserves special praise for his diligent work polishing the rough spots in the manuscript.

My bosses at the *San Antonio Express-News,* Steve Quintana and Al Carter, graciously gave me the leeway to finish the book. Thanks for your understanding, without which I wouldn't have been able to take on the project.

Bill Little, John Bianco, Thomas Stepp, and Jeremy Sharpe of the Texas sports information office helped me line up interviews of players and coaches and answered every request for rosters, play-by-play sheets, and other minutiae. Sheila Eveslage and David McWilliams of the Texas Letterman's Association were instrumental in helping me track down ex-players and coaches who helped tell the story. Enjoy retirement, Sheila.

One of the most daunting tasks proved to be rounding up the photos and illustrations. Jim and Susan Sigmon of the University of Texas were tremendously helpful in locating and providing images, from the colorful to the iconic. Without them this project would not have been possible. James Smith, photographer extraordinaire, provided many shots that captured the flavor of Texas football. Charlie Fiss of the Cotton Bowl pored through his photo files and provided many color images that hadn't seen the light of day in three decades. Ken Nordhauser's attention to detail helped round out the photo search. Larry Kolvoord kindly allowed me to use a photo that captured the essence of Earl Campbell at his best.

The staffs at the Center for American History at the University of Texas and the Austin Public Library's History Center deserve thanks for their help locating photos from the program's early days up until the Darrell Royal era. I'm also indebted to the photo editors at the *Arkansas Democrat-Gazette, The Dallas Morning News, The Oklahoman,* and *San Antonio Express-News* for their help in rounding up the right photos to tell the story.

Hurricane Katrina drove my sister-in-law Robin Stewart out of New Orleans and into my literary world, where she helped me out of many a jam when I had to be in two places at once. Michael Finkelstein, her son, proved to be a diligent researcher who helped fill in the gaps. Michael researched newspaper accounts of key moments in Longhorn history in the papers that told the story of the program, including all incarnations of the *Austin American-Statesman, Dallas Morning News,* and *San Antonio Express-News.*

If I have been able to add anything to the retelling of the glorious history of Texas football, it's because I've stood on the shoulders of giants. Lou Maysel helped guide a wet-behind-the-ears reporter on his first years covering the Longhorn beat at the *American-Statesman* in the mid-1980s, for which I'm eternally grateful. More to the point, he also produced two volumes of *Here Come the Longhorns,* an exhaustive and entertaining history of Texas football. Both were invaluable sources, as were works by authors Richard Pennington, Paddy Joe Miller, John Wheat, Jimmy Banks, Whit Canning, and Robert Heard.

Lou's son, Kent Maysel, graciously gave me access to his late father's photo collection, which proved invaluable. I miss Lou, and I hope this book in some way can honor his memory.

Kirk Bohls, whose knowledge of Texas football history is deep and formidable, went above and beyond by reading the manuscript and offering suggestions and corrections. Kirk also cowrote two books about Longhorn football, *Long Live the Longhorns* and *Bleeding Orange* with friend and former *American-Statesman* coworker John Maher. Both titles provided great background and insight.

Without the inspiration, support, and help from all mentioned here, the book would surely not have been possible. All credit goes to them. All blame for mistakes is mine and mine alone.

Throughout the process, my children kept asking me if I was done yet. Finally I have the answer Makala and Ben wanted to hear. Please accept my apologies for the games of kickball and catch missed. We can eat at Freebirds and play Mario Superstar Baseball now. But you've got to take Bowser.

To my wife, Barbara, I can say only that I'll never be able to pay you back for your patience and understanding during a process that was at times as difficult as it was rewarding. Now it's time to fulfill my end of the deal and clean my office. Soon. I promise.

University of Texas Sports Photography: 4, 6 12, 13, 14, 20 (bottom), 29 (top), 30, 31 (bottom), 33, 60, 62, 68, 83, 85, 88, 97, 106, 109, 113 (top), 114, 117, 119, 121, 129, 130, 132, 137 (bottom), 138, 140, 143, 149 (bottom left), 150, 166, 169, 177 (bottom), 178 (top and bottom left), 179 (top), 182, 187, 190, 193, 194, 195 (top), 197, 199, 200, 201, 203, 205, 206, 207, 208, 209, 211, 212, 213, 215, 217, 221, 228, 230, 233 (bottom), 234, 236, 241.

The University of Texas, Center for American History (Darrell K Royal Papers, Darrell K Royal Photo File, UT Football Photo Files, Walter "Buddy" Barnes Photograph Collection): 23, 32 (top and bottom), 40, 41, 43, 44, 47, 48 (top), 49 (top and bottom), 50, 51, 52, 54, 69 (top and bottom), 72, 77, 81, 87, 90, 94, 95 (top right), 146, 149 (top), 186.

James D. Smith: 9, 17, 19, 20, 21, 39, 99, 107 (bottom), 112, 116 (top and bottom), 133 (top and bottom right), 136, 137 (top), 156, 159, 174 (top and bottom), 177 (top), 183, 196, 202, 216, 218, 220, 222, 243, 244.

Cotton Bowl Athletic Association Archives: 48 (bottom), 57, 71, 73, 86, 91, 92 (top, middle, and bottom), 93 (top, middle, and bottom), 95 (top left), 96, 107 (top), 122, 126, 133 (bottom left), 170.

San Antonio Express-News: 3, 110, 115, 151, 153, 154, 188, 223, 225, 229, 232.

Austin History Center, Austin Public Library: 28, 29 (bottom), 33, 39, 67, 74, 75, 79, 149 (bottom right), 161, 163, 185.

Lou Maysel: 31 (top), 32 (middle), 36, 45, 65, 105, 162, 165, 168.

Ken Nordhauser: 4, 238, 239.

The Bryan-College Station *Eagle:* 152 (top and bottom).

Tournament of Roses Archives: 8, 233 (top).

Arkansas Democrat-Gazette: 168.

Cushing Memorial Library & Archive, Texas A&M University: 147.

Emory Bellard: 95 (bottom).

The *Dallas Morning News:* 125.

The *Oklahoman:* 128.

Mark Wangrin: 237.